01-07

CULTURES OF THE WORLD®

BOTSWANA

Suzanne LeVert

 Marshall Cavendish
Benchmark

New York

PICTURE CREDITS

Cover photo: © Martin Harvey, Peter Arnold, Inc.
AFP: 30, 34, 114, 115 • age fotostock / Andoni Canela: 75 • age fotostock / Art Wolfe: 78 • Alamy: 64, 117 • AP: 29, 36, 67, 97 • alt.TYPE / Reuters: 37, 39 • Aurora Photos: 66 • Bes Stock: 120, 130 • Corbis, Inc.: 6, 9, 12, 13, 16, 19, 24, 40, 43, 46, 50, 53, 54, 62, 72, 73, 76, 89, 92, 94, 98, 100, 102, 107, 108, 111 • Corel Stock Photo Library: 3, 10 • Karin Duthie / Illustrative Options / africanpictures.net: 30, 35, 86, 109, 116 • Getty Images: 6 (RF), 80 • Hutchison Library / Michael Kahn: 27, 51, 87 • Giacomo Pirozzi/ Panos Pictures: 5 • Jason Laure: 44, 77, 103, 110, 112 • Lonely Planet Images: 11, 14, 15, 52, 58, 59, 104 • Masterfile: 55, 91 • Minden Pictures / Frans Lanting: 1, 4, 8, 41, 57, 61 • National Geographic Image Collection: 129 • Stockfood / Aline Holsten: 131 • The Bridgeman Art Library: 18, 21, 22 • Audrius Tomonis/www.banknotes.com: 135 • Travel Ink: 56 • Tropix.co.uk/ M. Auckland: 42, 69, 71, 74, 79, 85, 105, 113, 119, 122, 124, 126, 128 • Tropix. co.uk/ J. Schmid: 125 • Tropix.co.uk/ J. Woollard: 32, 83, 118, 123, 127

PRECEDING PAGE
Women and children at the Okavango Delta pose with hand-made, conical baskets used for fishing.

Marshall Cavendish Benchmark
99 White Plains Road
Tarrytown, NY 10591
Website: www.marshallcavendish.us

© Marshall Cavendish International (Asia) Private Limited 2006
® "Cultures of the World" is a registered trademark of Marshall Cavendish Corporation.

Series concept and design by Times Editions
An imprint of Marshall Cavendish International (Asia) Private Limited
A member of Times Publishing Limited

All Internet sites were correct and accurate at the time of printing.

Library of Congress Cataloging-in-Publication Data
LeVert, Suzanne.
  Botswana / by Suzanne LeVert.—1st ed.
    p. cm.—(Cultures of the world)
  Summary: "Provides comprehensive information on the geography, history, governmental
    structure, economy, cultural diversity, peoples, religion, and culture of Botswana"—Provided
    by publisher.
  Includes bibliographical references and index.
  ISBN-13: 978-0-7614-2330-0
  ISBN-10: 0-7614-2330-3
  1. Botswana—Juvenile literature. I. Title. II. Series.
  DT2437.L482007
  968.83—dc22   2005032575

Printed in China

7 6 5 4 3 2 1

CONTENTS

The graceful impala is just one of the 164 species of mammals that can be found in Botswana. The name impala is a Zulu word, meaning "animal." Only mature male impalas have horns.

A Yei woman carries her young child on her back as she goes about her chores.

INTRODUCTION

BOTSWANA, a landlocked nation located in southern Africa, is considered one of the continent's shining success stories. Since attaining independence from Great Britain in 1966, Botswana has enjoyed nearly four decades of peaceful, democratic governance and benefits from a dynamic economy based on mineral extraction and, increasingly, tourism and other service-based industries. More than 17 percent of the country consists of protected wilderness inhabited by diverse animal, bird, and plant life, and people from all over the world enjoy safaris in Botswana every year.

Despite its natural and human resources, Botswana faces several challenges in the 21st century. Poverty and unemployment remain high, as do rates of HIV and AIDS infection. In order to safeguard their future, government agencies, the people of Botswana, and the international community must work together to solve these problems.

GEOGRAPHY

A LANDLOCKED COUNTRY slightly smaller than Texas, Botswana covers 231,743 square miles (600,370 square km) of southern Africa. Its bordering neighbors include Namibia to the west, South Africa to the south and east, and Zimbabwe to the north and east. Sections of Botswana's northern border touch on Zambia and Angola. Botswana spans about 600 miles (966 km) from north to south and 600 miles (966 km) from east to west. Rivers line three of Botswana's boundaries, the Molopo River on the south, the Limpopo along the southeast, and the Chobe and Shashi rivers in the northeast.

The country consists of three main environmental regions. The hardveld region consists of rocky hill ranges and areas of shallow sand cover in the east and southeast. Much of the rest of the country is covered by a deep layer of sand called the sandveld. Included in the sandveld is the enormous Kalahari desert, which extends into neighboring Namibia. The third region of the country, which is located in the northwest, consists of ancient lake beds in the base of the Kalahari basin. Most of Botswana's population lives in the hardveld region, which has the most fertile land in the nation. The country's largest cities are also located here.

Opposite: **Aerial view of the Okavango Delta.**

CLIMATE AND SEASONS

Botswana has a semi-arid climate, blanketed with hot, dry air throughout much of the year. Summer in Botswana lasts from October to March, when temperatures often rise to above 93°F (34°C). The air can be humid during the summer, especially in the morning when it ranges from 60 to 80 percent relative humidity. Relief from the heat of the sun frequently comes from the cloud cover and rainfall that occur during these months. Summer is also known for its high winds, when sand from the Kalahari blows across much of the country.

Much of the country is a plateau with an altitude of approximately 3,300 feet (1,006 m).

Dark storm clouds over the Okavango Delta. The rain mostly falls on summer afternoons.

Winter falls between April and September. It often gets cold enough for frost to develop at night, when the temperatures fall to below 37°F (2°C). The coldest month of the year tends to be June or July. Rain almost never falls during winter, and dry air and cloudless, sunny skies brighten winter days. These conditions make wintertime the most attractive season for both Botswana's magnificent wildlife that gather at watering holes and the tourists who come to view them.

Rain in Botswana is scarce, and therefore very precious. In fact, the Setswana word for rain is *pula*, which is also the name of the country's prime unit of currency. It also appears on the country's coat of arms. Drought has always been a regrettable fact of life for the people of Botswana. In the early 1980s, for instance, a severe drought swept across much of southern Africa, including Botswana. Just as the country began to recover, another drought occurred that lasted well into the 1990s. Botswana lost valuable crops and livestock in both incidents.

When it does rain, it comes in summer downpours that fall between November and April. Annual accumulations range from about 25 inches (640 mm) in the extreme northeast to about 5 inches (130 mm) in the extreme southwest. Brought in by winds from the Indian Ocean, rainfall tends to be erratic. Often a downpour may occur in one area, while another region just a few miles away remains dry.

Although water shortage is Botswana's usual challenge, areas of the country may flood during heavy rains. In 1995 heavy rainfall over most of the country resulted in flooding in parts of the Kweneng and Central Districts that caused 23 deaths and displaced more than 20,000 people.

THE KALAHARI DESERT

The world's largest continuous mantle of sand is the Kalahari desert, also known as the *Kgalagadi* (gall-ah-GA-DEE) in Setswana, the native language of Botswana. *Kgalagadi* means "the great thirst." The Kalahari is a large, arid to semi-arid sandy area that covers more than 193,000 square miles (500,000 square km) in southern Africa, including about 70 percent of Botswana. Altogether, the desert touches nine African countries south of the equator.

Vast areas of the Kalahari are covered by red-brown sands with no permanent surface water. However, the Kalahari is not a true desert because its annual rainfall exceeds the maximum rainfall normally experienced in a desert. In addition to the sands, the Kalahari also consists of a combination of grasslands, scrub, dry river beds, and dunes.

When it rains, water collects in dry valleys and salt pans, which are flat expanses of ground covered with salt and other minerals. If it were located

Above: **The tsessebe is the fastest among the antelope. They move in herds and enjoy grazing on open plains.**

Opposite: **The Okavango Delta in Botswana is considered Africa's largest and most beautiful oasis. It forms a natural refuge for the larger animals of the Kalahari, as well as wildlife usually not found in a desert, such as fish, crocodiles, and hippopotamuses.**

in a climate where the water did not evaporate faster than it accumulated, a salt pan would instead be a lake or a pond. The Makgadikgadi Pan in Botswana in the heart of the Kalahari is the largest salt pan in the country. In addition to holding vast quantities of salt, the Kalahari also holds deposits of other minerals, such as coal, copper, and nickel. The largest diamond mine in the world, the Orapa mine, is located in the northeastern Kalahari.

The Kalahari also boasts some of the region's largest and most highly stocked game preserves, including the world's second largest protected area, the Central Kalahari Game Preserve. Animals that live in the region include brown hyenas, lions, meerkats, antelope, and many species of birds and reptiles.

The Kalahari desert is the ancestral land of the Bushmen. Thought to be the first human inhabitants of southern Africa, the Bushmen—also called the San, or Basarwa—may have lived in the area for as long as 20,000 years. It should be noted that while there are many names for this group of people, "Bushmen" is commonly used as an all-inclusive name. In 2002 the Botswana government relocated all the Bushmen from these lands and placed them in fixed encampments. The Bushmen are now seeking legal action to allow their return to their ancestral homes.

RIVERS AND DELTAS

Geologists believe that water once flowed freely through what is now known as Botswana. Today, however, there are few lakes and rivers, and even these are not always flowing with water. Most rivers in Botswana are transient underground channels that rarely flow above ground except during the summer rainy season. Three of the largest rivers in Botswana are the Okavango River in the northwest, the Chobe River that forms the northern border with Zambia, and the Molopo River on the country's border with South Africa.

Described as "the river that never finds the sea," the Okavango River flows east into the arid sands of the Kalahari desert, where it disappears into a 6,000 square mile (15,540 square km) maze of lagoons, channels, and islands called the Okavango Delta. This delta is a remnant of the once great Lake Makgadikgadi, which was the largest inland sea in Africa before it began to dry up about 10,000 years ago. Less than 3 percent of the water emerges at the other end to fill Lake Ngami.

FLORA

Much of Botswana is covered by savanna, or grassland. In the southwestern part of the country, there is shrub savanna, while much of the rest of the country is covered in a mixture of trees and grass. There are small areas of forest, especially in the north along the Chobe River.

There are about 3,000 different species of plants in Botswana. One of the most common trees in Botswana is the baobab, known by its Setswana name *mowana*. Some *mowana* are more than 2,000 years old and their trunks measure more than 16 feet (5 m) at their widest. The bark of the *mowana* tree is slightly shiny and pinkish-grey in color. Its nickname is the "upside-down tree" because its branches resemble tree roots that appear to stick wildly into the air while its trunk plunges into the ground. Its large white blossoms appear from October to December, and it produces fruit with hard, grayish-brown coverings during April and May.

An important plant is the *tsama* melon, which provides an invaluable source of liquid for humans and animals. Cacti, aloes, and prickly pears, called *motoroko*, and a few species of evergreen tree are found on rocky hills. In the dry deciduous forest of the extreme northeast, trees such as the *mukwa*, or bloodwood, and *mukusi*, or Zimbabwean teak, are commercially exploited for timber.

FAUNA

Botswana is home to one of the world's greatest varieties of mammals, reptiles, and birds. These animals include some 164 species of mammals (including elephants, hippopotamuses, rhinoceroses, buffalos, zebras, leopards, and lions); 550 species of birds (including eagles, owls, falcons, flamingos, pelicans, herons, cranes, and swallows); 157 species of reptiles (including lizards, crocodiles, and pythons); 38 species of amphibians (including frogs and toads); and 80 species of fish (including tigerfish, tilapia, catfish, and carp).

Very large mammals such as giraffes, rhinoceroses, buffalos, and lions are generally confined to protected wildlife areas that cover about one-fifth of the country; hippopotamuses and crocodiles are generally found in the rivers and marshes of the north. Meerkats, a type of mongoose, are also common in the area. These small mammals are about one foot tall and have tan or gray fur, with dark brown bands and black-tipped ears and tail. They live in large social communities called mobs or gangs and are known to protect one another from their many natural predators. They keep watch by standing on their hind feet with their noses in the

Above: **Meerkats bask in the sun in the Kalahari desert.**

Opposite: **The baobab has a wide girth. The tree stores a large amount of water which makes the trunk appear swollen. Some species can grow to a staggering height of 130 feet (60 m).**

A magnificent African elephant and its calf in Chobe National Park.

air, poised to run if they spot an eagle or jackal looking for a snack.

A much larger mammal common to Botswana is the elephant. Unlike other parts of Africa where elephants represent an endangered species, there are perhaps too many elephants—about 120,000 of them—in Botswana. There are many reasons for this surplus. For instance, thousands of elephants migrated from nearby Angola as that country became ravaged by civil war. When another neighbor, Zimbabwe, closed its man-made waterholes, their elephant population also emigrated to Botswana. Finally, there are both internal and international anti-poaching policies that prevent the killing of elephants for their ivory tusks, which also increases the population.

Botswana is a haven for birdwatchers from all over the world, not only because of the many bird species who live or migrate there, but also because the flatness of the land and the sparse vegetation make bird watching so easy to do. The diversity of bird species is high not only in the national parks and reserves, but also throughout the country. For example, more than 400 species have been recorded in the highly populated capital city of Gaborone and its environs.

One of the country's most colorful avian species is the flamingo. There are two kinds of flamingos: the Greater and the Lesser. Greater Flamingos have a pink bill with black tip, and Lesser Flamingos have an evenly colored, dark purplish bill. The Lesser Flamingo is smaller and pinker than the Greater Flamingo. Both types can be found in large numbers at the Makgadikgadi Pans in the Kalahari desert.

GABORONE

With an estimated population of about 200,000, Gaborone is home to more than 10 percent of the country's population and is by far the largest population center in Botswana. It was founded as a district headquarters in about 1860 by African chief Gaborone Matlapin. In 1885 Gaborone became the capital of the British protectorate, Bechuanaland, and remained the capital when Bechuanaland became independent as Botswana in 1966. Now a modern city boasting world-class shopping malls, international hotels, and office parks, Gaborone is located in the southeast of Botswana along the Notwane River.

Gaborone was chosen as the capital largely because it lies close to the railway line and has ready access to water. Today, it is also served by the Sir Seretse Khama International Airport, located about 25 miles (17 km) from the city. In addition to its position as a transportation hub for the region, Gaborone's proximity to nearby manganese and asbestos mines makes the city an important industrial center.

Gaborone also acts as the country's administrative center. Public officials meet in the Government Enclave, a series of buildings that house the National Assembly and other national government agencies, and foreign embassies. The United States Embassy is located near the Enclave, as is the Orapa House, where Botswana's diamond wealth is sorted, packaged, and sent out to the markets of the world.

Gaborone has become an important center for regional economic and political development. The Southern African Development Community (SADC), headquartered in Gaborone since its formation in 1980, works to increase economic cooperation among its members, including Angola, Lesotho, Malawi, Mozambique, Swaziland, Tanzania, Zambia, and Zimbabwe, in addition to Botswana.

As is true for most modern cities, Gaborone has experienced an increase in its crime rate as its population has grown and congestion swelled. In 2005 the U.S. Department of State rated Gaborone as a high crime area, particularly for armed robbery and home invasion. By far, however, vehicle accidents are the most serious safety threat affecting residents and especially tourists unfamiliar with the area. It is not uncommon for drivers, especially those driving local taxis and mini-buses, to stop, change lanes, or pull into traffic without looking. Running red lights and "jumping" green lights are also very common practices among local drivers. All drivers run the risk of hitting both domestic and wild animals on the road after dark.

HISTORY

THE MODERN NATION of Botswana is a striking success story on the continent of Africa. One of modern Africa's most stable and vibrant nations, Botswana also has a rich cultural and political history. It remains home to the region's first settlers, the San of the Kalahari desert who have lived in its semi-arid climate for centuries and maintain a cultural and political presence today. Also played out in Botswana was a struggle between the European powers for the colonization of southern Africa. For decades a protectorate of Great Britain, which means that Botswana retained control over its internal affairs to some extent while Great Britain provided military and economic protection, the country won its independence in 1966. Since then, it has prospered as a strong democracy.

EARLY INHABITANTS

Evidence exists that people inhabited the area now known as Botswana as early as 17,000 B.C. These early dwellers were ancestors of Khoisan-speaking hunters and herders, whose descendents include the present-day Bushmen. Eventually the Khoisan people adapted their way of life to include seasonal migration in family groups over grasslands and wetlands to more fertile soil. In the last centuries B.C., many Khoisan also herded sheep and cattle near the Okavango Delta and the Makgadikgadi lakes.

Although ancestors of the Bushmen were first to inhabit the area, they were joined by Bantu-speaking people who traveled from the south and east at the beginning of the common era.

From around 1095, the southeastern part of the country saw the rise of a new culture, the Moritsane, ancestors of the Kgalagadi chiefdoms. The Moritsane raised cattle and hunted. The Toutswe people, who also herded cattle, dominated east-central Botswana between about 700 and 1200.

Opposite: **The cave paintings at the Tsodilo hills date back to as early 17,000 B.C.**

Based on findings at Tsodilo Hills, an archaeological site in northwestern Botswana, it appears that the early settlers also subsisted by hunting and fishing. Primitive mining tools found at the site indicate that in about A.D. 850, another group of Bantu speakers arrived and became the region's first miners.

A Zulu warrior dressed for battle.

GREAT MIGRATIONS

During the mid-13th century, a large group of Bantu speakers moved south of central Africa and settled in the area now known as the Transvaal Province of South Africa. The ancestors of the Tswana—Botswana's largest present-day population group—were among this migration. By the early 1700s, many of these people had moved again in search of food and water, this time into what is now Botswana. As they settled, they broke up into smaller groups, and each established its own culture and traditions. The Tswana groups and the Bushmen lived in relative harmony during this period, even as the first Europeans began to visit the coast of southern Africa.

THE DIFAQANE

From about 1750 onward, disruptive changes began to occur among several southern African societies. Collectively called the Difaqane, or Mfecane, which mean "the crushing," these disturbances took place largely because climate changes, including a drought that caused a shortage of grazing land, triggered competition for water and food between the different groups sharing the region. In addition, African groups were also contending with white settlers for land and resources as the ivory, cattle, and slave trades spread inland.

The largest and most powerful African group to emerge during this period was the Bantu-speaking Zulu. During the mid-19th century, its ruler, Shaka, came to dominate most of eastern South Africa. Among those who fled to land occupied by the Tswana groups was one of Shaka's most powerful chiefs, Mzilikazi of the Ndebele group.

THE RISE OF THE KGOSI

During and following the wars of the Difaqane, the Tswana groups formed into cohesive, organized groups, called *merafe* (mer-raf-ee). Each individual group, or *morafe* (moor-af-ee), had its own chief, or *kgosi* (plural *dikgosi*). Each *kgosi* (ko-see) led his own group and did not owe allegiance to any other authority. The position of *kgosi* was inherited,

THE LOUVRE OF THE DESERT

Attractive rock paintings found in northwestern Botswana, near the border of Namibia, offer clear evidence that the nation now known as Botswana was inhabited as long ago as 17,000 B.C. A cluster of five hills, the Tsodilo Hills preserves a chronological account of human activities and environmental changes over at least 100,000 years.

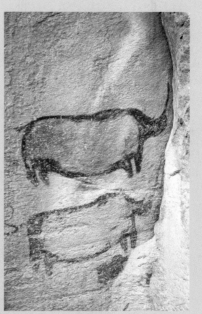

Nicknamed "the Louvre of the Desert," this World Heritage Site presents one of the highest concentrations of rock art in the world, with more than 5,000 individual paintings and hundreds of carvings. The work of the Bushmen who populated the region during the Middle and Late Stone Ages (about 100,000 and 70,000 years ago, respectively), most of the paintings depict the animals that the Bushmen hunted, including elands, giraffes, and rhinoceroses.

Excavations of the Hills also exposed tools and other implements used by these first settlers, including what are perhaps the oldest fish hooks discovered in southern Africa. Tools made of stone, wood, and bone were unearthed. This proves that the Bushmen hunted and gathered to survive. The Tsodilo Hills represent a sacred place to the Bushmen, who believe that they are not only the site of the world's creation, but that they serve as a resting place for all ancestors.

normally passing from father to son. On the death or retirement of a *kgosi*, his eldest son would automatically succeed to the throne. If the eldest son were still too young to assume the power, his uncle would rule as *motshwareledi* or regent.

Under the *dikgosi*, these communities competed with one another to trade with southern Africa along new roads that were built to traffic ivory, gold, and diamonds. As well as allowing trade to flourish, however, these roads also brought European missionaries and explorers to the interior.

Two of the first, and arguably most influential, missionaries were Robert Moffat, who settled with the Tlhaping in about 1820, and later his son-in-law, David Livingstone, who lived among the Kwena after about 1843. Both men taught some English and Christian tenets; they also acted as intermediaries between rival groups and some European colonists.

THE BRITISH AND THE DUTCH

The two main groups of European settlers in South Africa were the Dutch, also known as Afrikaners, and the British who fought a long battle for dominance over southern Africa. In 1836 some 20,000 Afrikaners began moving north from Cape Colony to avoid British rule and settled to the north of the Vaal River, near modern Botswana. Helped by groups of Tswana—and by missionary Robert Moffat—the Afrikaners were able to resist and then defeat the Zulu chief Mzilikazi of the Ndebele group. After their victory, however, the Afrikaners laid claim to the land and attempted to enslave the Tswana.

Once the Tswana realized that they would be allowed to stay on the land only if they worked as laborers on Afrikaner farms, they looked to the British for help. The British agreed to protect the Tswana, especially after the Afrikaners attempted to annex much of the valuable land around

In 1652 the Dutch established the first European settlement in the region at Cape Colony in what is now South Africa. Until 1806, when the British arrived and took control, the Dutch were the primary European settlers in the region.

the Limpopo River, which forms the border between present-day South Africa and Botswana. In 1880 the First Afrikaner War between the Boers and the British began. It reached a climax about six months later at the Battle of Majuba Hill, when the Afrikaners soundly defeated British forces on February 21, 1881.

After their victory, the Afrikaners continued to push toward what is today Botswana. The Tswana people, anxious to retain as much independence as possible, looked to the British to protect them once again. After appeals for assistance by the Tswana leader, Khama III of the Ngwato group, the British government put the newly named Bechuanaland territory under its protection in 1885 and promised self-rule to the Tswana. Although the Tswana groups retained some degree of independence under this arrangement, smaller groups, including the San and Herero, were largely left out of the process.

This painting shows one of the many battles fought between the Dutch and the British during the Afrikaner Wars.

THE ROAD TO INDEPENDENCE

Within just a few years, the Tswana and others living in the region found themselves threatened by yet another force. The British placed responsibility for the development of the territory largely in the hands of Cecil Rhodes and his British South Africa Company (BSAC). Rhodes was a British financier who already had earned millions in the diamond mines of South Africa. His ambition then became to build a railroad that extended from the Cape Colony in the south across the continent to Cairo, Egypt in the north. He also wanted to bring all of Bechuanaland under his control, but he met with strong resistance from the Tswana and other groups living there.

A painting of Cecil Rhodes (1853–1902) during one of his encounters with the Zulus in South Africa.

In 1895 Khama III and two other local *dikgosi* traveled to London to negotiate with the British. They persuaded the colonial secretary, Joseph Chamberlain, to promise that Great Britain would continue to protect their independence. In return, they transferred ownership of a strip of territory for construction of Rhodes' railway to the north. Between 1894 and 1897, Rhodes built a 400-mile (644-km) stretch of his railroad, which extended from Mafeking, the capital of the protectorate, to Bulawayo in present-day Zimbabwe.

Although the British did indeed protect Bechuanaland from both the Boers and the BSAC, they also retained control over the Tswana and other groups living in the protectorate. In 1891 the British government designated two commissioners to oversee the region, one in South Africa's city of Cape Town and the other in Bechuanaland's capital of Mafeking, located, oddly, within South Africa. The order mandating this policy stated that "chiefs were now responsible to the British and not to their subjects." Thus the *dikgosi* were no longer able to exercise complete authority over their groups, but rather had to govern in association with the commissioners. In addition, the *dikgosi* were forced to collect taxes from their people to pay the British.

In 1910 the Union of South Africa was formed as an independent country to Bechuanaland's south. It consisted of four states inhabited by the British and Afrikaner populations who lived in the region following the Second Afrikaner War, which ended with the defeat of the Afrikaners in 1902. These white settlers were ruthless in their pursuit of power and domination over the black majority living in the new country.

The people of Bechuanaland were just as eager to remain free from South Africa as they had been to avoid Afrikaner control. Fortunately, despite pressure from South Africa to cede Bechuanaland, Britain refused.

As late as 1935, the British government confirmed that it would not transfer sovereignty of the protectorate to South Africa without the agreement of the people of Bechuanaland.

LEADERSHIP EMERGES

The *dikgosi* of the eight major clans of Tswana attempted to govern their own people within the protectorate. However, they were often met with reprisals from the British. Starting in 1918, for instance, Sechele II ruled the Bakwena clan. Sechele II was a traditional ruler who had spent time working outside of the protectorate in the mines of South Africa. He urged his people, and members of other groups, to resist becoming a part of South Africa. He also fought for more power for the *dikgosi*. His popularity among his own people and other Tswana clans threatened British control. In 1931 the British forcibly removed Sechele II from office and sent him to jail, where he died eight years later.

Another important leader of this period was Tshekedi Khama of the Bangwato. In 1925 he began to lead the group as regent because the rightful *kgosi*, Seretse Khama, was only four years old when the prior *kgosi*, his father Sekogma II, died. Like Sechele II of the Bakwena, Tshekedi had experienced segregated life in South Africa and fought against transferring Bechuanaland to South African rule. For the 25 years he acted as regent, he struggled to maintain the independence of the *dikgosi*.

The rise of the National Party in South Africa in 1948 and its aggressive pursuit of apartheid further strengthened British opinion against incorporating Bechuanaland into South Africa. Instead, Britain began to work in earnest with the Tswana toward political and economic self-sufficiency. In 1950 the government created a Joint Advisory Council

Seretse Khama with his wife Ruth Williams and their children at home in Croydon, Britain.

consisting of colonial administrators and the *dikgosi*. Beginning in 1952, a political movement urging independence for the protectorate began to organize. The head of the movement was Seretse Khama, grandson of Khama III.

Seretse proved to be an interesting choice for a new leader. His uncle Tshekedi, who acted as his regent until he came of age to become chief, had sent Seretse to Britain to study at Oxford University as a youth. There, he met and married Ruth Williams, a British white woman. This interracial marriage deeply troubled not only his uncle, but also the government of South Africa, which had introduced apartheid laws against sexual relations between different races. Under South African pressure, the British banned Seretse Khama and his wife from returning to Bechuanaland. Six years later, following much negotiation, the British allowed Seretse to return as a private citizen. Although he remained banned from inheriting the *dikgosi*, he stood ready to lead his people through the next phase of their history.

INDEPENDENCE FOR BOTSWANA

About eight years after Khama's return, pressure among the people of Botswana for total independence reached a climax. Finally, Britain granted Bechuanaland internal self-government in 1965. A year later, on September 30, 1966, the country attained full independence as the nation of Botswana. Sereste Khama was elected the country's first president.

The world Botswana faced at independence was a difficult one, both internally and externally. Its African neighbors were in turmoil. South Africa's policy of apartheid denied the entire black majority population the right to vote and forced them into ethnic reservations the government called "homelands."

There were different homelands for each South African group, including the Zulu, Xhosa, and others. By separating the groups, the South African government hoped to prevent the people from uniting against the regime.

In the late 1990s, Botswana became involved in a water dispute with Namibia, which sought to divert water from the Okavango Delta to its drought-stricken cities. Had Namibia's claim succeeded, it would have threatened the Delta, home to a diverse wildlife population that attracts about 75 percent of Botswana's tourists. In December 1999 the International Court of Justice ruled in favor of Botswana.

Rhodesia, the country now known as Zimbabwe, also had a white-dominated, repressive regime in the years following Botswana's independence. From 1971 to 1979, Rhodesia became embroiled in a bitter civil war as its black majority fought to overthrow the ruling elite. Operating from bases in neighboring Zambia and Mozambique, the rebels made periodic raids into Rhodesia. Refugees from the war also fled to Botswana, where they were harbored in refugee camps.

Although Botswana disapproved of both Rhodesia and South Africa's policies, the country needed to maintain good political relationships in order to promote trade, as well as to preserve access to other parts of the continent on neighboring roads and railways. Nevertheless, during the 1970s, Botswana allied itself with other independent nations, particularly Zambia and Tanzania, to become one of the "Front Line States" promoting majority rule in Rhodesia and South Africa.

MODERN BOTSWANA

In addition to the challenges Botswana faced within the region, it also confronted a number of internal problems. A five-year-long drought that began just before independence continued to undermine the livelihoods of its citizens. One of the first items on the government's agenda was to establish and fund famine relief programs for the thousands of Batswana—the name used to define citizens of Botswana—who lost their cattle and their crops.

As well as responding to this immediate crisis, President Seretse Khama also proposed an aggressive and ambitious long-term agenda, which included bringing democracy to the people of Botswana, developing the country's resources, and encouraging self-reliance and unity for all Batswana. These were grand goals indeed, considering that at the time

of independence Botswana was one of the poorest nations in the world. Few schools existed and the country only had about two miles (3.2 km) of paved road. It had a per capita annual income of just $100 and its people relied almost entirely on subsistence agriculture to survive. In the early years of independence, Botswana's government remained financially dependent on Britain to cover the cost of administration.

But in 1967, a mineral find changed life forever for most of the people of Botswana. An enormous store of diamonds was discovered at Orapa, an area located at the edge of the Kalahari desert. Botswana's economy grew by leaps and bounds. Throughout most of the next two decades, its economy grew between 12 and 13 percent every year.

In the meantime, between 1984 and 1990, Botswana suffered when South Africa raided the country in retaliation for their support for anti-apartheid movements. Two raids on the capital city of Gaborone by the South African army in 1985 and 1986 killed 15 civilians. In 1994 regional turmoil largely ceased after South Africa held its first free elections.

A statue of Seretse Khama stands outside the National Assembly building in Gaborone.

REFUGE FROM TURMOIL

Dukwe Camp, located in the plains of northeastern Botswana, was established in 1978 by the Lutheran World Federation to cope with a massive influx of refugees from Rhodesia, now known as Zimbabwe, and South Africa. At one time, the camp was home to more than 45,000 men, women, and children who fled oppression and racism in these nations. Other refugees arrived from Angola, which experienced Africa's longest and bloodiest civil conflict after the country attained its independence from Portugal in 1975.

The government of Botswana attempted to maintain the camps for strictly humanitarian and non-military purposes. The camps provided refugees with shelter and other assistance, and military activities were strictly prohibited. Refugees who wanted to work or study outside the camp were required to obtain written permission from the government.

Nevertheless, from the safe haven offered by the Dukwe Camp, many of today's African leaders planned the future of their countries. One of those who stayed in the make-shift huts and tents of Dukwe was Barry Gilder, now South Africa's Director-General of Home Affairs in charge of refugee issues. Although the flow of refugees from southern Africa stopped after Zimbabwe and Namibia achieved independence (in 1980 and 1990, respectively) and South Africa ended apartheid in 1994, the camp remains home to about 3,500 people from 14 other African countries.

Politically, Botswana has remained a stable democracy since independence, with free and peaceful elections taking place every five years. Since Seretse Khama became the country's first president, the Botswana Democratic Party (BDP) has received the majority of votes in both presidential and assembly elections. However, in the 1994 elections, the opposition party, the Botswana National Front, gained a significant voice in the legislature for the first time. The following year, public discontent over high unemployment and other problems sparked riots in Gaborone.

In 1997 the constitution was amended to reduce the voting age from 21 to 18, to extend the franchise to Batswana living abroad, and to limit future presidents to a total of 10 years in office. Later that year Quett Masire announced that he would retire as president on March 31, 1998. His vice president, Festus Mogae, replaced him until his term was over; Mogae was then elected to his own first five-year term. In 2004 the people of Botswana re-elected him.

As Botswana entered into the 21st century, it continued to face formidable challenges. Although its economy is still strong, Botswana is planning to

diversify its economy. Diamond mining has become more and more mechanized and thus employs fewer and fewer people. Indeed, many Batswana must depend on subsistence farming to survive.

Perhaps the greatest threat to the future of Botswana, and indeed the health of the entire continent, is AIDS. This deadly disease, caused by infection with the HIV virus, reached epidemic proportions during the 1990s. Although Botswana has promoted one of the most aggressive AIDS treatment and prevention plans in the world, the cost to the economy and to the population in terms of human suffering remains incalculable. More than one in three Botswana men, women, and children suffer from AIDS. How Botswana faces the future depends greatly on how it responds to its AIDS crisis, as well as how it continues to expand its economy. Certainly, with care, its stunning physical beauty and abundance of wilderness and wildlife—so rare in the modern world—will attract tourists to Botswana and provide much pleasure to its citizens for decades to come.

U.S. president George W. Bush visited President Mogae in Gaborone in July 2005 to boost trade relations as well as offer support for the country's struggle against AIDS.

KHAMA III   SEBELE I   BATHOEN I

GOVERNMENT

SINCE INDEPENDENCE in 1966, Botswana has been a free and open democracy, one of the few on the African continent. Its government is a parliamentary republic. A popularly-elected National Assembly elects the president, who in turn appoints a cabinet. The president wields executive power; it is his or her job to enforce the laws enacted by the National Assembly. The vice president is part of the president's cabinet, which is also part of the executive branch of government. Administratively, the country is divided into ten districts.

In 2003 the World Economic Forum ranked Botswana the least corrupt country in Africa. The Swiss-based organization graded each nation in the world based on the rule of law, evidence of corruption, and enforcement of contracts. A poster at the Gaborone Airports warns newcomers of its strict anti-corruption policy. It reads: "Botswana has ZERO tolerance for corruption. It is illegal to offer or ask for a bribe." The country is an active member of the international community, with seats in the United Nations and the African Union, among other organizations.

ELECTIONS

Elections for the legislative branch of government—the National Assembly— take place every five years. Botswana's electoral system is "first past the post," or FPTP, which means that the candidate who wins the majority of the votes in his or her constituency wins the seat, just as occurs in the United States. The president is head of state and indirectly elected. Following the parliamentary elections, the presidential candidate of the party with a majority of elected Assembly members assumes office.

Once in office, the president appoints a cabinet of ministers from among members of parliament, though some non-elected persons may be appointed under special circumstances. The cabinet consists of a vice

Opposite: **A national monument in Gaborone dedicated to the three *dikgosi* (chiefs)— Khama III, Sebele I, and Bathoen I—who successfully persuaded the British to protect the sovereignty of Botswana in 1895.**

The country's constitution, referred to as Molao Mothe or "the law that establishes all law" in Setswana, was enacted in 1966.

31

president and a flexible number of ministers and assistant ministers. Festus Mogae was re-elected in October 2004 for a second term. Limited by the constitution to 10 years in office, Mr. Mogae says he will step down in 2008, just before the next general elections.

Botswana is a multi-party democracy. However, one party, the Botswana Democratic Party (BDP), has been in power since independence and was re-elected most recently in 2004. Several opposition parties contested the BDP in the last election. The BDP's principal challenge came from the Botswana Congress Party (BCP) and the Botswana National Front (BNF), which is an ally to two other parties, the Botswana People's Party and the Botswana Alliance movement. About 77 percent of the population

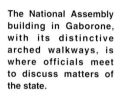

The National Assembly building in Gaborone, with its distinctive arched walkways, is where officials meet to discuss matters of the state.

voted in the 2004 election; the BDP won 44 seats, the BNF 12 seats, and the BCP one seat. The next elections are due in 2009.

Despite the peaceful nature of the elections, and the fact that universal suffrage gives everyone in Botswana over the age of 18 the right to vote, many people in the country question the fairness of the electoral system on a number of grounds. First, there is no public funding of political parties in Botswana, which makes it difficult for those without funds to run for office. Second, many voters are unhappy with the FPTP system and believe that proportional representation would be more appropriate. Proportional representation involves the election of more than one person in each district and divides the seats of each district according to the proportion of votes cast for each party that runs a candidate for office. Thus if the candidates of a party win 50 percent of the vote in a 20-member district, they receive 10 seats; if another party wins 20 percent of the vote, they receive 4 seats, and so on. Many Batswana feel that this method would assure a more fair representation of all the parties in the country. In 1999, for example, the BDP won 54.3 percent of the vote, but obtained only 33 percent of the 40 seats in parliament.

Another proposal under consideration is the direct election of the president. The parliament, which has been made up overwhelmingly by BNF party members since independence, elects the president. Many voters would like to change the constitution so that voters cast a separate ballot for president in the 2008 election.

Finally, citizens are also reconsidering a 1996 constitutional amendment that allows for the automatic succession of the vice president if the acting president leaves office before his term expires. The prior constitution allowed for such an event, but did not establish a specific time limit for which a new president should be elected.

For more than 30 years after independence, the voting age in Botswana was 21. In 1997, however, the people of Botswana voted to reduce the age to 18. Today, suffrage is universal for those 18 years and older, except for prisoners or people who are mentally incapacitated.

THE PRESIDENT

Botswana's president is Festus Mogae *(right)*. He was born in Serowe, which is Botswana's largest village located in a fertile, well-watered area in the country's central region. He received his college education in England, where he received an undergraduate degree from Northwest London Polytechnic, an honors degree in economics from Oxford University, and a degree in developmental economics from Sussex University.

He returned to Botswana in the late 1960s, shortly after the country became independent. He joined the Botswana Democratic Party as one of the many young educated politicians eager to help create a new country. In 1968 he served as a planning officer in the Ministry of Finance and Development and Planning, where he was promoted three times until 1972. Starting in 1975, he served as secretary to then president Quett Masire. This position enabled him to serve on the boards of DeBeers Botswana Mining Company (later renamed Debswana), the Bank of Botswana, and the International Monetary Fund. In 1989 the president appointed him Minister of Finance and Planning. In 1992 he was elevated to the post of vice president. He succeeded President Masire in 1998 and was re-elected in 2004. Rumors are rife that he intends to resign a year before his term expires in 2008 so that his vice president, Ian Khama, will succeed him, ensuring that the BDP retains national power.

Known to be "no nonsense" when it comes to governing his country, President Mogae has concentrated on developing new programs to meet the health and educational needs of the country's citizens. Of special concern are Botswana's alarmingly high rate of AIDS transmission and the medical and social challenges connected with the virus. He has also promoted the expansion and privatization of the country's telecommunications and transportation industries. According to a 2004 survey, less than half of the country's population had confidence in President Mogae's administration, and yet more than 80 percent re-elected the BDP party in 2004.

THE LEGISLATURE

Botswana has a bicameral parliament consisting of a 15-member House of Chiefs and a National Assembly. The House of Chiefs is made up of the *dikgosi*, the leaders of the eight major tribes recognized at independence, three elected sub-chiefs, and three members selected by the other 12 members. The role of the House of Chiefs is to advise the National Assembly on matters of custom, culture, and tradition. They have no voting or veto power, but instead act as an advisory board to parliament. All bills affecting tribes or tribal property and customary law must be reviewed by the House before discussion in parliament. Each member of the House must be at least 21 years of age and be fluent in English. He or she cannot have been active in politics for the previous five years or work for the government in any capacity.

A 2004 bill introduced in parliament attempts to address discrimination against smaller ethnic groups. Currently, all eight of the chiefs are Setswana-speaking people. The bill would give permanent seats in the House of Chiefs to smaller ethnic groups, including the !Kung (KOON). Although the role of the House of Chiefs is primarily advisory, it can summon a cabinet minister to answer questions about his or her government work.

The National Assembly is made up of 57 members popularly elected and four appointed by the majority party. All members serve five-year terms. Officially, the assembly controls government expenditures and approves the government's major decisions. The National Assembly is responsible for choosing the president after legislative elections. The president then chooses a cabinet from the National Assembly.

The parliament of Botswana consists of a House of Chiefs and a National Assembly.

In 2005 about 18 percent of parliamentary members consisted of women.

A LEADER NAMED "WOMAN"

In December 2003 Mosadi Seboko *(right)* made history when she became the first female chief in Botswana. Like her father before her, she became the leader of the Balete royal family, but not without first having to fight against her own family's efforts to keep the chiefdom a patriarchy, a system by which only males may inherit power and position.

Seboko's first name *Mosadi* means "woman" in Setswana. According to Seboko, it was the word her father uttered in surprise when his firstborn child turned out to be a girl and not a boy who could easily inherit the throne. When Seboko's father died in 1966, her uncle became chief, then her only brother succeeded him in 1996. When he died in 2001, her father's relatives put forward a male cousin as successor. But Seboko insisted that the patriarchy of the tribe was merely custom and that Botswana's constitution guarantees equality among men and women.

With support from her mother, seven sisters, and women's rights activists around the country, Seboko became chief of the Balete. She balances her duties as chief with those of a mother: She has four daughters that she has raised alone since she divorced their father.

LOCAL GOVERNMENT

Following independence, local government was introduced across the country, consisting of 10 district councils, three town councils, two city councils, and one township authority.

Local governments cooperate with local organizations, such as the *kgotla*, or village assembly, and village development committees (VDCs). The *kgotla* is a traditional institution for communication between the government and the community, while the VDCs undertake local improvement activities in the villages.

Dikgosi continue to enjoy respect in rural communities and have been integrated into the modern public administration. The *dikgosi* preside over *kgotla*, where community matters are discussed. They collaborate with councils and district commissioners to create plans for regional development. The local government also has direct control over fire protection; kindergarten, pre-school, and primary school matters; gas and heating services; and the economic promotion of its ward.

THE LEGAL SYSTEM

Botswana has a dual legal system that combines foreign law (Roman Dutch Law) for major crimes with customary law, which governs everyday disputes and property rights among the rural tribes. Botswana's courts are considered to be fair and free of political interference. Trials are usually public and those accused of the most serious crimes are provided public defenders. Civil cases, however, are sometimes tried in customary courts, where defendants have no right to legal counsel. Prisons are overcrowded, prompting the government to build new facilities in recent years.

The judiciary is the third arm of the government, working side by side with the executive and legislative branches. Under the constitution of 1966, it is mandated "to do justice in accordance with the constitution of Botswana, as by law established and in accordance with the laws and usages of Botswana without fear or favor, affection, or ill will." Judges are appointed by the president on the advice of an independent Judicial Service Commission, as established in the constitution.

The judiciary is divided into the magistrate courts, the High Court, and the Court of Appeal. The magistrate courts have original jurisdiction over all offenses except capital crimes such as murder, treason, sedition, or attempts to commit these crimes. These courts are empowered to pass sentences of corporal punishment. The High Court, headed by a chief justice appointed by the president, supervises the proceedings of the magistrate courts. All appeals from the customary courts and magistrate

Two !Kung file a lawsuit against the Botswana government at a court in Ghanzi. Botswana's legal system is based on Roman-Dutch law and indigenous customary law.

Opposite: **Botswana and French Special Forces enter a building during a joint military exercise.**

courts are heard in the High Court. Aside from jurisdiction over capital crimes, the High Court also has the power to decide on any question about constitutional law. The Court of Appeal has jurisdiction over criminal and civil cases arising from the High Court. The president appoints the chief justice of the Court of Appeal. The remaining justices of the appeal court are appointed by the president based on the recommendation of the Judicial Service Commission.

Prosecution of all legal actions for and against the government is initiated by the Attorney General's Office. Under the Constitution and the Criminal Procedure and Evidence Act, the Attorney General is empowered to direct all criminal prosecution. For minor offenses, the Botswana police and the Directorate of Corruption and Economic Crime are also authorized to prosecute for and on behalf of the Attorney General. The basic statute for prosecuting criminal cases is the penal code.

THE OFFICE OF THE OMBUDSMAN

Established by the Ombudsman Act of 1995, the office of the Ombudsman investigates complaints of government corruption or injustice that is brought by any citizen of Botswana. If the office finds merit in a complaint, it first addresses the matter with the specific agency or official involved. If the agency or official refuses to cooperate, the Ombudsman makes a special report of the issue to the National Assembly. The Ombudsman also has jurisdiction over human rights violations as well as grievances from individuals in legal custody.

The office of the Ombudsman is "extra-ministerial," which means it is not under the direction or control of any other person or governmental office or agency. The president appoints the Ombudsman for a period of four years and he or she can only be removed for misconduct.

THE MILITARY

When Botswana achieved independence in 1966, it had no standing army. At the time, the government chose not to establish a national army and, for 11 years, Botswana depended on a paramilitary police force for its defense. However, due to the internal strife experienced by its neighbors Zimbabwe and South Africa, and the increasing intrusions of those countrys' insurgents into Botswana's territory, a decision was made to create an army.

In 1977 an act of Parliament established the Botswana Defense Force (BDF) consisting of 132 men drawn from the police force. The Deputy Police Commissioner, Mompati Merafhe, was appointed commander of the new force. The president chose as the second-in-command 24-year-old Ian Khama, who would later become his vice president. The BDF contained five light infantry units, a reconnaissance company, an air force, and several smaller units.

Since then, the BDF has grown considerably. Today, it has grown to just over 12,000 personnel, and its ground forces consist of three infantry brigades and an armored brigade. The Botswana Defense Air Force Arm consists of about 500 men. The government spends about $228 million of its annual budget to support the BDF.

ECONOMY

BEFORE ITS INDEPENDENCE in 1966 Botswana was one of the poorest countries in the world. Since independence and the discovery of the country's vast mineral reserves, Botswana has become one of the most economically vibrant and successful countries in Africa. In fact, according to the U.S. Department of State, Botswana has had the fastest growth in per capita income in the world since its independence. The country is one of the world's largest producers of diamonds, which account for more than 80 percent of Botswana's export earnings. The country's abundant wildlife enhances the tourist industry, which represents another major economic sector.

Above: **Women on their way to fish with woven baskets. Most Batswana use such traditional tools rather than modern fishing gear.**

Opposite: **Tourists sit near a campfire in Chobe National Park. Wildlife and wilderness are the main attractions for tourists to the country.**

Today, the government is eager to diversify its economy and attract more foreign investment. Textiles, agriculture, tourism, and financial services industries all offer opportunities for growth. Two major investment services rank Botswana as the best credit risk in Africa.

On the other hand, not all the news is good for Botswana. Despite its relative wealth, its people still suffer from high rates of poverty. Although the official unemployment rate in 2005 was 23.8 percent, less than a quarter of the adult work force participates in formal paid employment.

Furthermore, the AIDS epidemic continues to take a terrible economic and social toll on the country. As of October 2005, Botswana has the second highest rate of HIV/AIDS infection in the world after Swaziland. The cost of treating the illness and coping with the loss of men and women during the prime of their economic lives affects every sector of the economy. As Botswana struggles to come to terms with this disease and its consequences, the country also hopes to continue to diversify and develop its economy in the years to come.

A copper-nickel mine in the mining town of Selebi-Phikwe, southwest of Francistown.

MINING

Today, mining contributes 34.2 percent of the country's gross domestic product (GDP) and 50 percent of its tax revenues. This is a far cry from the time of Botswana's independence, when mining contributed just 1 percent to the country's GDP. This remarkable increase is due to the development and discovery of several major diamond deposits, primarily in northern Botswana.

Now the world's leading diamond producer in terms of the quantity and grade of its diamonds, Botswana also has significant copper, nickel, cobalt, gold, soda ash, and coal deposits which are currently being explored and developed. Today, Botswana's mining industry provides employment for approximately 13,000 people.

DIAMONDS EVERYWHERE

The boom in Botswana's mining industry began in the late 1960s, when the South African company DeBeers discovered quantities of garnet and other stones indicative of the presence of diamonds in northern Botswana. In 1967 the largest diamond pipe in the world was discovered at Orapa, located northeast of the Central Kalahari Game Reserve.

DeBeers quickly entered into a partnership with the government of Botswana to form the Debswana Diamond Company Ltd. Today, Debswana owns four major diamond mines in Botswana. The first mine began production at Orapa in 1972, followed by Lethlakane in 1975, then Jwaneng in 1982, and Damtshaa in 2003. In December 2004 Debswana negotiated 25-year lease renewals for all four of its mines with the government of Botswana.

The Debswana output for 2004 was a record 31 million carats, making Debswana the world's leading diamond producer by value and volume. Exploration for other sources of diamonds in the country continues.

Botswana earns about one billion dollars a year from the diamond industry, which forms the backbone of its economy. The country is the largest producer of gem diamonds in the world, but it also produces industrial diamonds, which are used in many manufacturing processes. The hardest substances on earth, diamonds are used in industrial settings, such as to prevent machine parts from rubbing against each other and wearing down.

Inside a Debswana diamond mine.

THE DIAMOND MINES

Its name is derived from a Greek word meaning "impossible to tame," and it is a mineral renowned for its hardness and its ability to disperse light. These properties make diamonds valuable both for jewelry and industrial purposes.

Most diamonds are mined from subterranean geological structures called volcanic pipes. Volcanic pipes form when volcanoes erupt deep within the earth. Pipes are composed mainly of two rock types, kimberlite and lamprolite. The intense pressure and high temperatures found in the pipes help to form the diamonds.

The world's largest mine, Botswana's Orapa mine *(below)*, is an open pit mine. Open pit mining is used when deposits of minerals are found near the surface of the earth. When minerals are located deep within the earth's layers, tunneling into the earth is required to extract the gems.

The first step in open pit mining involves removing the subsoil from the pipe with large hydraulic shovels. Explosives and drills break apart hard rock, which is then removed with heavy equipment. This stage of mining can take some time. In the mine at Jwaneng, for instance, it took two years to remove the top layers of soil before actual mining began. Once digging starts, miners extract kimberlite and lamprolite in levels or tiers, starting from the top and working into the earth. From each tier, the ore is taken to plants for further processing.

In the past several years, Botswana has further diversified with its diamond industry by establishing several diamond cutting and polishing factories. In 1993 a state-of-the-art diamond cutting and polishing facility, with both automated and manual equipment, opened in Molepolole. A subsidiary of the largest manufacturer of diamonds in the United States, Lazare Kaplan Botswana (LKB) now employs about 200 Batswana. The government of Botswana is represented on LKB's board of directors and owns 15 percent of its shares.

OTHER MINERALS

Another large mining company is Bamangwato Concessions Ltd. (BCL), which also works in partnership with the Botswana government. BCL operates a copper-nickel mine at Selebi-Phikwe, located about 62 miles (100 km) southeast of Francistown. Production in this mine began in 1974. About 95 million tons (86 million tonnes) of copper-nickel ore deposits exist in this area. With nearly 5,000 workers, the plant is one of the nation's largest employers.

Botswana has many other smaller deposits of minerals. Morpule Colliery, the country's only coal mine, is situated near Palapye and operated by the Anglo American Corporation. Gold was discovered and mined early in the country's history, and a number of mines continue to operate today. Crushed stone and sand as well as limestone are quarried for use in road building and the construction sector. Semi-precious stones are also collected and processed. Other minerals known to exist in Botswana include antimony, chromite, feldspar, fluorine, graphite, gypsum, kaolin, lead, manganese, platinum, silver, talc, uranium, and zinc.

AGRICULTURE

About one-half of Botswana's population lives in rural areas and depends largely on subsistence farming for survival. Although more than 80 percent of the population is involved in farming or the cattle industry, the agricultural sector supplies only about 50 percent of the country's food needs and accounts for only 3 percent of its GDP.

Cattle herding has long been one of the core elements of Botswana's economy and cultural heritage. Throughout their history, Batswana measured wealth by the number of cattle they owned. It remains the country's most important agricultural sector. Today, Botswana exports

Another mineral important to Botswana's economy is soda ash. The plant at Sua Pan uses the natural carbonate resources of Botswana to make this product, which is utilized in glass manufacture, detergents, and general chemical manufacture. The Sua Pan plant also has the capacity to produce 650,000 tons (589,700 tonnes) of salt per year for use as a raw material in the production of certain chemicals.

Tourists enjoy a ride in a motor boat along the channels of the Okavango Delta.

more than 95 percent of the beef produced to international markets, particularly to South Africa and the European Community.

Only 6 percent of the country's semi-arid land is arable, and only 1 percent is cultivated each year. The country's main commercial crops are corn, sorghum, and animal feed plants. The Botswana-owned company known as Sefalana (meaning "the bountiful granary" in Setswana) has long maintained its position as the leading wholesaler and grower of these crops. The company owns mills at Lobatse, Pilane, and Serowe.

TOURISM

Thanks in large part to its remarkable landscape and the wide variety of wildlife that inhabits it, tourism is an increasingly important industry in Botswana, accounting for almost 12 percent of the GDP. In 1999 about 840,000 tourists visited Botswana. By 2004 more than 1.1 million people arrived, representing a 7.7 percent growth in five years. In 2004 tourism generated $365 million for Botswana's economy.

About 85 percent of visitors to Botswana come from the neighboring nations of Zimbabwe, Namibia, and South Africa. Most other tourists come from Great Britain, the United States, and Germany. By far the most popular destinations in Botswana are its many game reserves and national parks, which occupy about 17 percent of Botswana's total area. An additional 20 percent of the land is designated as wildlife management areas.

More than 60 percent of Botswana's highways are now paved.

TRANSPORTATION AND COMMUNICATIONS

Connecting 1.6 million men, women, and children who live in Botswana to one another, to people in other countries, and to information from around the world has often proved a challenge in this sparsely populated country. Today, however, Botswana boasts extensive highways, several airports, and an increasingly extensive telecommunications industry.

A paved highway connects all the major towns and district capitals in the country, while the Trans-Kalahari Highway connects Botswana to the port of Walvis Bay in Namibia.

The country's main airport is Sir Seretse Khama International Airport, located nine miles (17 km) north of Gaborone. Named after Botswana's first president, it has a terminal building containing a currency exchange, a restaurant, and duty-free stores. Another international airport is located near Francistown in the northeast. Three domestic airports and 108 airfields dot the nation.

Botswana is a landlocked nation, so it depends largely on neighboring countries to receive and distribute its imports and exports. Goods can be conveniently transported by road to and from countries in the Southern African Customs Union (SACU) region within hours. Founded in 1969, the SACU is the oldest customs union in the world. Its aim is to maintain the free interchange of goods among its member countries.

FRANCISTOWN

Home to more than 90,000 people, the second largest city in Botswana is located in northern Botswana, close to the border with Namibia. Affectionately called "the old lady of Botswana," Francistown is the site of the region's first gold rush. Although it still retains a frontier town feel, it is now a center of commerce and industry. Its population has doubled in just the last decade. It is now known as the "Capital of the North," thanks in large part to its status as a transportation center, with all the country's main roads passing through it, its small airport, and railway lines.

Industries established here include the manufacture of gaskets, clothing, knitwear, shoes and accessories, textiles, ceramics, and chemicals. Numerous service industries flourish, particularly those related to the construction and transportation trades.

Botswana has one of the most modern telecommunications infrastructures in Africa. A fiber optic telecommunications network now connects all major population centers. There are more than 160,000 telephone lines connected, resulting in about seven lines per every hundred people. Even more Batswana, about 435,000, use cell phones. The growth of mobile cellular service and the country's participation in regional telecommunications systems are helping to expand this sector of the country's economy.

GETTING THE NEWS

Botswana's constitution guarantees freedom of speech and expression and, generally speaking, those rights are respected by Botswana's government. The government-owned Botswana Press Agency provides most of the information to media agencies owned and operated by the state, including the free *Daily News* newspaper, which publishes in Setswana, the most widely-used native language. In addition to the government-owned newspaper, Botswana has an active, independent press made up of seven weekly newspapers and two privately owned radio stations.

Radio is the most important medium of public communication. Although the government monopolized radio broadcasting in the past through its nationwide Radio Botswana, two private stations now broadcast in five of the country's 10 largest cities. In 2000 the government launched Botswana Television, the country's only national television station.

Although the constitution guarantees freedom of speech and expression, there are certain media laws that work to restrict independent journalism in Botswana. In particular, the National Security Act of 1986 has come under fire for the control it gives the government over press activities. Adopted at the height of South African aggression toward Botswana's support of anti-apartheid activists, the Act has been used to charge seven people with publishing information the government has classified as secret.

INTERNET

Internet use in Botswana continues to increase with about 20,000 Batswana now connected to the World Wide Web. Botswana Telecommunications Corporation is the main Internet Service Provider and for a long time enjoyed a monopoly in that area. In 1996 the government passed a bill that made it easier for competitors to enter the market. Today, there are about six Internet Service Providers that offer all services such as e-mail and domain name registration. Many people in urban centers have access to Internet cafes. An estimated 30,000 Batswana use the Internet.

In September 2005, the government radio station, Radio Botswana, joined the Internet age when University of Botswana computer science staff made its broadcasts available over the Internet. That means that Batswana living outside the country can listen to news and music from home—all broadcast in Setswana, the national language.

ENERGY

The government's primary energy organization, the Botswana Power Corporation, recently produced an advertisement that depicted a woman

In 2005 community leaders proposed a Mass Media bill to the Botswana government that, according to Botswana's Deputy Permanent Secretary in the Communications, Science, and Technology Ministry, Lucky Moahi, seeks to "ensure that journalists do their work professionally and maintain standards to curb biased reporting."

A wind wheel in the Kalahari desert. A rotor in the structure converts the force of the wind into mechanical energy and from that electricity.

in a reed hut using an electric iron to press her clothes. Throughout much of Botswana's history, the idea of electricity fueling an iron or other appliance located outside of a major city or town seemed far-fetched. Until recently, only about 30,000 homes enjoyed electricity. Today, however, the country is coming closer to wiring even its most remote villages.

In 1995 the government entered into an agreement with 12 other southern African nations, called the Southern African Power Pool, which seeks to provide reliable and affordable electricity to all of its consumers. Villages in Botswana's Okavango Delta, for instance, receive their electricity from the Namibian power utility company, NAMPOWER, while the Chobe District gets its power from the Zambia Electricity Supply Corporation. Botswana's southwestern Kgalagadi District is supplied by one of South Africa's largest power companies, Eskom.

THE ECONOMIC IMPACT OF AIDS

There is no question that Botswana has one of the most successful economies in Africa and has experienced an impressively steady economic growth for more than four decades. However, the impact of Botswana's high rates of AIDS infection on the health of its economy cannot be underestimated.

There are two major effects an AIDS epidemic has on a country's economy: a reduction in the labor supply as so many young adults are infected, and increased costs in medical care and lost work time due to illness. AIDS also has an impact on every sector of the economy. The loss of even a few workers during crucial periods of harvesting and planting, for instance, can significantly reduce the size of a harvest, and thus diminish income from agriculture. In fact, it is estimated that Botswana will lose at least one-fifth of its agricultural workers to the epidemic. Furthermore, many households in Botswana rely on farming small plots of land simply to survive. If the person who maintains the garden becomes ill or dies from AIDS, the rest of the family will suffer as well. Even banking and other service industries suffer when AIDS strikes a country as badly as it has hit Botswana, the loss of key employees combined with the increase in health costs can devastate companies.

In order to minimize both human suffering and economic devastation, the Botswana government launched one of the most aggressive AIDS treatment and prevention programs in Africa in 2001. Called Masa, which is the Setswana word for "new dawn," the program offers the latest antiretroviral therapy to AIDS patients on a nationwide basis, a first in Africa. The success of the initiative to individual families as well as to the country's economy is as yet unknown, but more and more Batswana receive treatment and education every day through this massive effort.

ENVIRONMENT

BOTSWANA'S NATURAL WILDIFE is both bountiful and fragile. Although the variety and quantity of its flora and fauna is among the most diverse and plentiful on the continent, human activity in the region has threatened the country's natural habitats, putting both the animals and the land at risk.

With only seven people per square mile (2.6 square km), Botswana remains one of the most sparsely populated countries in Africa. Nevertheless, beginning in the 1980s, the Botswana government formally recognized the need to protect and preserve the country's wide range of wild animals and plants. In December 1990 the National Assembly of Botswana approved the National Conservation Strategy (NCS). One of the NCS' priorities is to make sure that the government and the people recognize the effects of economic development on the environment.

The NCS also works with regional and international environmental organizations, including the African Wildlife Foundation and the United Nations, to protect Botswana's bio-diversity. As President Mogae told the African Wildlife Foundation in November 2003, "A key aspect of [Botswana's] conservation efforts is the acceptance of the reality that wildlife knows no boundaries."

Above: **A brightly colored road sign warns motorists of crossing elephants.**

Opposite: **Dawn breaks on the savanna of central Botswana. The country's breathtaking landscapes and diverse wildlife are major draws for nature-loving tourists.**

AGRICULTURAL DIVERSIFICATION

The NCS is seeking ways for Batswana to diversify from cattle production to other industries less damaging to the country's wildlife and land resources. Raising cattle over so much of the nation's rangeland has dramatically reduced the once plentiful wildlife of the country's plains and disrupted the migratory patterns of many species.

Cattle feeding at a trough. Such cattle drives take up large areas and may deprive other wildlife of potential habitats.

Although only constituting a small percentage of the country's gross domestic product, cattle ranching has always been an important part of Botswana's cultural and economic landscape. Until the 19th century, all cattle were the property of a tribal chief, who allocated cattle for herding and for the production of milk for herders and their dependents. The chief helped establish control mechanisms to regulate livestock numbers and manage the rangelands.

In order to ensure that cattle received enough water in this semi-arid land, Tswana cattle owners and colonial officials invested in new technology to develop boreholes, which are deep wells with motorized pumps. The creation of boreholes expanded the amount of land available for grazing and cattle production. In 1936 rangelands accounted for about 20 percent of Botswana's land areas. By 2004 this figure had risen to more than 45 percent.

During the 1950s, markets for Botswana meat in Great Britain and Europe developed. The need to encourage these markets led to the development of large-scale, privately owned ranches and slaughterhouses. It also led to the construction of veterinary fences to separate quarantine zones in order to control disease, particularly Foot and Mouth Disease. Environmentalists believe that these fences cause much loss of wildlife throughout the country because they also impede the wild animals' natural migration.

In 1975 the government established the Tribal Grazing Land Policy (TGLP) in order to address what had become a significant threat to

Botswana: overgrazing and rangeland degradation, particularly on tribal lands. The TGLP divided tribal land into three zones: commercial land, where exclusive rights were granted to individuals and groups; communal land, in order to promote better management; and reserved areas, consisting of unallocated land set aside for later use by the poor. Later, a fourth zone was added, establishing wildlife management zones in which domestic stock is permitted but wildlife is protected.

Despite these efforts to better manage the land involved in cattle herding, significant problems remain, including the loss of productive land through desertification.

A saddle-billed stork stops at Linyati Swamp in the Chobe National Park.

DESERTIFICATION

Desertification is the process by which productive land becomes non-productive, usually because of mismanagement. Desertification occurs mainly in semi-arid areas that border on deserts, like Botswana.

In Botswana, overgrazing by cattle is the major cause of desertification. Grazing animals that move in response to patchy rainfall eat the plants in the area. In addition, the use of fences to quarantine cattle has prevented animals from moving in response to food availability, resulting in overgrazing in the enclosed areas.

According to the Botswana Rangelands Inventory and Management Project, about 17 percent of the country's rangeland is now degraded. In order to reverse this trend, the government has ratified a number of international conventions, including the United Nations Framework Convention on Climate Change, the Convention on Biological Diversity, and the United Nations Convention to Combat Desertification. Another

MOVEMENTS OF PRODUCTS INTO AND OUT OF NGAMILAND
PRODUCTS NOT ALLOWED TO LEAVE NGAMILAND
1. FRESH MEAT EXCEPT FROM BMC IN AN APPROVED TRUCK ACCOMPANIED BY A VETERINARY PERMIT
2. LIVE CATTLE
PRODUCTS ALLOWED TO LEAVE OR ENTER NGAMILAND WITH A VETERINARY PERMIT
1. BILTONG 2. POULTRY 3. MILK/MADILA 4. REAMS (DIKGOLE) 5. FISH
6. LIVE SHEEP AND GOATS AFTER 3 WEEKS QUARANTINE
7. HAY 8. HIDES AND SKINS 9. PETS HORSES AND DONKEYS ETC
PRODUCTS ALLOWED TO LEAVE OR ENTER NGAMILAND WITHOUT A VETERINARY PERMIT
1. AGRICULTURAL PRODUCE FOR HUMAN CONSUMPTION (WATER MELONS SWEET REED MAIZE ETC)
2. THATCHING GRASS 3. MAST AND BASKETS
4. ANY PROCESSED COOKED MEATS FOR DIRECT HUMAN CONSUMPTION
5. PROCESSED ANIMAL FEEDS 6. FIRE WOOD
NOTE FRESH MEAT CAN ENTER NGAMILAND WITH A VETERINARY PERMIT ALL THE ABOVE EXCEPT LIVE CATTLE CAN MOVE FREELY WITHIN NGAMILAND WITHOUT A VETERINARY PERMIT

A billboard at a veterinary quarantine point informs drivers of restrictions on the transportation of specific food items, bulding materials, and animal products.

organization, the Desert Margins Initiative is a group of nine countries—Botswana, Burkina Faso, Mali, Namibia, Niger, Senegal, Kenya, Zimbabwe, and South Africa—that works with local groups to identify ways to combat desertification, including rehabilitating the land, rotating grazing areas to allow vegetation to recover, and enforcing rules about logging.

PROTECTING FORESTS AND TREES

Concerted efforts are made to conserve and regenerate Botswana's valuable but ever-diminishing forests. Overgrazing by livestock has denuded part of the country of trees, notably in the south and around the larger villages. Tree plantation programs are helping to alleviate this problem, at the same time that they increase public awareness of trees as both protectors of the environment and providers of useful products.

WILDLIFE

National parks and game reserves take up more than 17 percent of the country's land. Here, all commercial farming and hunting are prohibited. A further 22 percent of the country is designated as Wildlife Management Areas, where wildlife is given priority and strict controls on commercial activities are imposed.

Nevertheless, drastic reductions in the wildlife population have occurred during the last 30 years. Almost 80 percent of the wildebeest and zebra populations, for example, were lost during the 1980s, largely due to the significant loss of land to livestock grazing, poaching and overhunting, the growth in human population, and drought.

THE RHINOCEROS

Botswana's rhinoceros population remains among the most fragile of its species, despite the size of the species and its long history in Botswana.

Game reserve wardens hold up confiscated elephant tusks. Although the large and uncontrolled elephant population hurts crops and forests, sometimes even injuring people, the authorities are wary that lifting the animal's protected status may fuel the black market for tusks.

The white rhinoceros is the largest of its species and, compared to the black rhinoceros, it is less aggressive and tends to move slowly.

Until hunters ravaged the herds, many white and black rhinoceroses lived in northern Botswana. Although the black rhinoceros was always rare, the white rhinoceros population was once widespread and common in this area. As a result of indiscriminate sport hunting, however, both species were reduced to very low numbers. In recent years, efforts by the Botswana government, collaborating with a host of regional and national organizations, have brought both species of rhinoceros back to the country in greater and greater numbers.

In 1967 the first four white rhinoceroses were reintroduced to Botswana. Between 1974 and 1981, the government reintroduced a total of 71 white rhinoceroses into Chobe National Park and 19 into Moremi Game Reserve. Unfortunately, although these numbers should have been enough to sustain and increase the herd, all but 19 white rhinoceroses were killed by poachers by 1992. The government then developed a strategy to conserve the white rhinoceros by capturing as many surviving white rhinoceroses as possible and transporting them to protected sanctuaries, such as the Khama Rhinoceros Sanctuary and the Mokolodi Private Game Reserve. In August 2004, the first white rhinoceros calf was born in the wild, 16 months after its mother was released. Today, approximately 30 white rhinoceroses live in Botswana.

In 1992 the black rhinoceros was considered locally extinct. In 1993 the government brought four black rhinoceroses from South Africa and released them into the Okavango Delta. Efforts continue to ensure the survival of this species in Botswana and throughout southern Africa.

THE FASTEST ANIMAL ON THE PLANET

In 2003 the Botswana government established the Cheetah Conservation Botswana (CCB) to study the cheetah in Botswana. As of the start of the century, experts estimate that the cheetah population in Africa has declined by as much as 90 percent, making it one of the continent's most endangered cats. CCB hopes that its studies will reveal new ways to protect this remarkable species.

Able to run at speeds that top 60 miles (97 km) per hour, the cheetah is by far the fastest animal on land. The name cheetah comes from the Hindi word *chita*, meaning "spotted one." Tall and slender, with evenly-spaced spots on cream-colored fur, these animals have bodies built for speed, with long, thin, muscular legs. Adults measure about 44 to 55 inches (112 to 140 cm) from head to rear and stand 26 to 37 inches (66 to 94 cm) at the shoulder.

Once found throughout Africa and Asia, the number of cheetahs and the places they inhabit have steadily declined. In 1952 cheetahs were declared extinct in India, and they have not been seen on the Arabian Peninsula since 1950. Their disappearance can be traced to uncontrolled hunting by humans for sport and for trade in cheetah skins. Farmers in areas inhabited by the cheetah also often kill the animal to prevent them from feeding on domestic livestock. Botswana's CCB is a sister organization of Namibia's Cheetah Conservation Fund, an international conservation organization that has worked with the Namibian government, local communities, and farmers to promote sustainable cheetah populations since 1990.

THE GAME RESERVES

Large tracts of Botswana's land area has been set aside as national parks and game reserves. From the lush green in the Okavango Delta in the north to the red sand dunes in the southwest, great expanses of wilderness are home to the country's remarkable variety of flora and fauna. Here are just a few examples.

CENTRAL KALAHARI GAME RESERVE The second largest game reserve in the world is situated in the center of Botswana. It is characterized by vast open plains, salt pans, and ancient riverbeds. The Bushmen have resided within the area of the reserve for thousands of years. Originally nomadic hunters and gatherers, the Bushmen, also known as the !Kung, now live in settlements, largely within the southern half of the reserve.

A famous part of the reserve, called Deception, was a camp set up by two British citizens, Mark and Delia Owens, to study the wildlife there, particularly the brown hyena and the black-maned lions. The book they wrote about their experiences there, *Cry of the Kalahari*, made the area famous. Today, the Owens Foundation supports wildlife research in Botswana and other parts of Africa, as well as in North America.

CHOBE NATIONAL PARK The second largest national park in Botswana, the Chobe National Park offers one of the greatest concentrations of wildlife found on the African continent. Animals are present during all seasons of the year, sometimes in great numbers. If visitors stay in the park for more than a day or two, they are likely to get a chance to see all of the animal species who live there, including giraffes, impalas, tsessebe (springboks), roan, sables, wildebeests, kudus, buffalos, waterbucks, elands, lions, hyenas, jackals, and cheetahs, among others.

Animals may move from one reserve to another when seasons change and food and water in one place cannot sustain them.

Chobe National Park has four distinctly different ecosystems within it: hot, dry hinterland in the center of the park is surrounded by lush plains and dense forests in the extreme northeast, marshland in the southwest, and swamps in the northwest.

A flock of spotted sandgrouses fly past an African elephant.

KHAMA RHINOCEROS SANCTUARY Established in 1992 to protect rhinoceroses and to revive an area that once teemed with wildlife, this sanctuary is located near Serowe in central Botswana. Serowe is one of the largest traditional villages in Africa and is the birthplace of Botswana's first president, the late Sir Seretse Khama.

The central feature of the park is the Serowe Pan, a large, grass-covered depression with several natural water holes. This pan serves as a prime habitat for the white rhinoceros and other grazing animals, such as giraffes, zebras, and jackals. To date, 14 white rhinoceroses have been relocated into the sanctuary.

MASHUTU PRIVATE GAME RESERVE Located between the Limpopo and Shashe rivers, this game park is the largest private reserve in southern Africa. It also boasts the largest elephant population (almost 900) on private land in the world. The elephants here are known as the relic herds of Shashe, which once roamed the Limpopo Valley but became extinct in the area for almost 60 years until 1947.

But elephants are not the only wildlife here. Lions, leopards, baboons, cheetahs, and giraffes are among the many species that make this area their home. One of the reserve's prime attractions to wildlife lovers are its night tours, which allow visitors to view night predators on the prowl, such as leopards and other wild cats.

BATSWANA

BOTSWANA'S FIRST HUMAN INHABITANTS settled in the land more than 50,000 years ago. Their history is one that includes civil wars, devastating droughts, colonization, and a successful struggle for independence. Botswana's borders were created by the British colonial rulers with very little regard to the geographical distribution of languages or ethnic groups. Hence, many people who share culture, history, and language with Botswana also reside in other African countries, particularly South Africa, Namibia, and Zimbabwe.

The country's population is dominated by people who speak a Bantu language called Setswana. Known as Tswana, they make up about 80 percent of the population. Small minorities of Kalanga, Herero, !Kung, and other groups also live in Botswana, along with a few thousand people of European extraction. The people of Botswana call themselves Batswana (singular, Motswana). Although the term Batswana originally referred only to Setswana speakers, it has come to mean all the people who live in Botswana.

Although the country remains a peaceful democracy, tension continues to exist between the majority Tswana and the smaller groups, particularly the Kalanga and the !Kung. Many members of these groups feel that the Tswana has dominated the culture of Botswana and denied them some of their rights. Non-Setswana speaking groups are not consulted on decisions affecting their lives through the *dikgosi*, nor are their languages used in education or in the media. In 2001 the Botswana High Court found that certain sections of Botswana's constitution and at least two of its domestic laws discriminate against minority groups. The government is working to redraft those sections. A recent government-ordered displacement of Bushmen from their homeland in the Kalahari desert has brought these tensions to the forefront.

Opposite: **A Herero woman and her grandchild outside their home.**

THE TSWANA

Making up most of Botswana's population, the Tswana are believed to be descendants of King Mogale, the "brave one" in Setswana. Mogale lived in the Magaliesberg Mountains in South Africa's Gauteng Province during the 14th century. Mogale and his people eventually migrated northward to establish themselves in Botswana.

Once one large clan, the Tswana broke into smaller groups called *merafe* (mer-raf-ee), or chiefdoms. Over many generations, the *merafe* split into several branches. Eight of those branches form the eight major Tswana groups living in Botswana. Under the country's Chieftainship Act, these groups include the Kwena, Ngwato, Ngwaketse, Tawana, Kgatla, Tlokwa, Rolong, and Tlhaping. The Tribal Territories Act distributes all the land in the country to these eight groups.

Tswana children in a village in southern Botswana.

The Kwena, the Ngwato, and the Ngwaketse of Kanye, a town in southern Botswana, are the three largest groups of Tswana in Botswana today. Although there remain differences among these groups, they speak very similar dialects of Setswana and have common traditions and religious beliefs. Each *morafe* can be identified by its totem, or emblem, usually of an animal or plant. People never kill, eat, or use the skins of their totems. The Kwena honor the *kwena*, or crocodile, the Kgatla honor the *kgabo,* or monkey, and the Ngwato venerate *phuti*, the antelope.

Although most Tswana now live in larger cities and towns conducting business, running the government, and living relatively urban lives, a great number still live in traditional villages. Their daily lives remain focused on taking care of livestock and growing and preparing food.

HOME AWAY FROM HOME

Among the homelands created by the apartheid government of South Africa in 1971 was Bophuthatswana, established as a home for all Tswana-speaking people who lived in South Africa. Totaling 17,000 square miles (44,000 square km), the homeland consisted of seven enclaves dispersed over the former South African provinces of Cape Province, Transvaal, and Orange Free State. Mmabatho, its capital, was situated in an area near the border of Botswana. Bophuthatswana was designed so that the South African government could exclude the blacks from the national political process.

Economically and politically, the homeland depended on South Africa for survival, since no other country recognized the homelands as independent states and only South Africa had "diplomatic" relations with them. In 1985 Bophuthatswana had a population of 1.6 million, many of whom worked as migrant workers in South Africa. In 1994 South Africa's new constitution abolished its apartheid policy and reabsorbed the homelands and their people into the country.

Today, more Tswana live in South Africa than in all of Botswana, a country named for them. About three-quarters of the Tswana live in South Africa and only a one-quarter in Botswana.

A group of Kalanga women perform a traditional dance.

THE KALANGA

The largest non-Tswana group is the Kalanga, who live mainly along the Zimbabwe border just near Francistown. With a population of about 160,000, the Kalanga are ethnically diverse; some are related to the Ndebele people of Zimbabwe and South Africa, and others to the Zulu nation. The Kalanga, whose language is known as iKalanga, make up about 11 percent of Botswana's population.

Today, there are three major groups of Kalanga in Botswana: the Lilima, the Nyayi, and assimilated groups of people, including some Setswana speakers who became part of the Kalanga group after migrating to Kalanga territory. The traditional Kalanga way of life has always differed sharply from that of the Tswana. Instead of forming large villages based on raising cattle, the Kalanga still inhabit smaller farming settlements and keep cattle only for social and religious purposes. Many Kalanga travel between Francistown and their villages, working in the city while maintaining their farms. The Kalanga have become successful business people and government officials.

THE BUSHMEN

Also known as the !Kung, !Kung San or the Basarwa, the Bushmen consist of several different groups who speak languages that belong to seven linguistic families. At one point in their history, the Bushmen numbered several million, but today only about 100,000 Bushmen live in southern Africa. About 60,000 live in Botswana, while the others primarily abide in Namibia, South Africa, and Zimbabwe. Until recently, about 4,000 Bushmen maintained a traditional existence, living much as their ancestors had, in Botswana's Central Kalahari Game Reserve (CKGR).

Africa's "first people," as the Bushmen are sometimes called, have long struggled to maintain their way of life in southern Africa. About 4,000 years ago, waves of cattle-raising Tswana from central Africa moved south and pushed the Bushmen deep into the dry Kalahari desert. The arrival of white settlers in the 1600s brought further dispossession of land, enslavement, and even slaughter. Among the most discriminated against and abused, the Bushmen survived only by virtue of their remarkable skills as hunter-gatherers and their tenacity as a culture.

By the time Botswana won its independence in 1961, only about 60,000 Bushmen remained in the country. Most of them lived in remote government settlements in seven of the country's nine national districts, with only about 3,000 residing in their ancestral homelands in the CKGR. During the mid-1980s, the Botswana government began efforts to remove the Bushmen from the CKGR and place them into existing or new settlements outside the reserve. The government claimed that the !Kung way of life,

Roy Sesana is the founder of the First People of the Kalahari, an organization that works for the rights of the Kalahari Bushmen in Botswana. Sesana was awarded the Right Livelihood prize in Sweden in December 2005 for his efforts.

Herero women wear ankle-length dresses with long bodices, complete with elaborate headdress. This costume was adopted from German missionaries who arrived in Namibia in the 19th century.

which had evolved to include the hunting of horses with firearms, had begun to interfere with the wildlife in the park. In addition, social services, such as public education and health care, were difficult to deliver to the nomadic people across such a large expanse of land.

However, the Bushmen and their supporters claim that the government and the powerful DeBeers diamond mining company had located a new source of precious gems in the Kalahari, and wanted the land in order to mine more of the country's most important source of revenue.

In 1997 more than 1,700 Bushmen were removed to live in other settlements, while the remaining 700 stayed behind. Since that time, the Bushmen and the Botswana government have been struggling—in court and on the Kalahari—over control of the land and its resources. In 2004 a court case brought by the Bushmen against the government was dismissed by the court due to a technical error. As of May 2006, the Bushmen and the government were still litigating the issues in court in what is now considered the longest and most costly trial in Botswana's history.

THE HERERO

The Herero are a pastoral group known for their large cattle herds and their distinctive clothing. Numbering just over 100,000 in total, most Herero live in Namibia, with about 25,000 calling Botswana home. They arrived in northwest Botswana in 1904, after being driven out of Namibia by German colonists. Most Herero live in small farming communities, though many of them split their time between their farms and work in the nearby city of Francistown. Like the !Kung and other minority groups, the Herero are not recognized as an ethnic group by the Botswana Constitution or the Tribal Territories Act, and so, according to a 2004 U.S. Department of State report, "remain marginalized in the political process."

THE WHITES

Today, about 15,000, or 1 percent, of Botswana's population are white people. Most whites immigrated to Botswana from South Africa, although many come from Europe and the United States. Working largely in mining and other industries, most of Botswana's white population lives in Gaborone, Francistown, and other industrial centers.

CIVIL RIGHTS FOR ALL BATSWANA

In 2005 a bill that would amend Botswana's constitution was introduced to the parliament. Although the bill would allow the eight Setswana-speaking groups to continue to designate their traditional leaders to the House of Chiefs, it mandates the election of 20 representatives from eight other minority groups. The amendment also allows the president to appoint

Despite the government's efforts, cases of physical violence against women, including sexual assault, continue to rise. Acts of sexual violence are sometimes tantamount to a death sentence, considering that HIV-infections have reached epidemic proportions in the country.

five additional members to the House, increasing the total from 15 to 40. The 20 additional representatives from non-Tswana groups, including the Kalanga, the Herero, and the !Kung, would be selected by district electoral colleges, to be chaired by a civil servant appointed by the Minister of Local Government. However, many members of minority groups remain unhappy with the provisions of the Constitutional Amendment Bill because they feel that discrimination against minor groups has not been addressed in it.

WOMEN

Another group of people who are working toward greater equality are Batswana women. Currently, improvements are made through the rigorous efforts of non-government organizations, such as the Emang Basadi Women's Association in Gaborone and the Metlhaetsile Women's Infomation Centre in Mochudi. The Ministry of Labor and Home Affairs has also set up a Women's Affairs Department to look into the well-being of women, in areas such as education, employment, and legal representation.

Making up more than half the country's population, Batswana women face considerable discrimination that arise from traditional practices. For instance, a women who marries under traditional customary law has no right over property and cannot enter into contracts without her husband's consent. Now, with education, more and more women are choosing to marry under an intermediate traditional law, which recognizes their right to shared property. As for civil law, the government passed the Abolition of Marital Powers Act in 2004. This act gives the wife equal control over the property and guardianship over the children.

In the workplace, Batswana women have considerable success in professional jobs. Advancement to senior management positions, however, is much harder, as is the case for women pursuing political careers. This is linked to the deep-rooted perception that women do not belong in the public domain.

Women come out in their colorful dresses and shawls to attend a wedding celebration, which is often filled with joyous song and dance.

LIFESTYLE

MANY PEOPLE IN BOTSWANA have moved from rural villages to small towns and cities. Roughly half of the nation's population works and lives in towns such as Palapye, Mahalapye, Selebi-Phikwe, and Francistown, and particularly in Botswana's growing capital city, Gaborone. Most of the people live in the eastern part of the country where there is sufficient water and fertile land. The !Kung, or Bushmen, were moved from their ancestral lands in the Kalahari desert to resettlement areas in 1997.

Botswana is a sparsely populated country. Although it compares in size to the state of Texas, Botswana has just 2.7 people per square mile (2.6 per square km), while Texas manages to fit nearly 80 people into that same area. According to statistics gathered by the U.S. Central Intelligence Agency in October 2005, the median age of Batswana is about 19 years, while in the United States, the median age is 36. In 2005 infant mortality in Botswana was 54 deaths per 1,000 births, while in the United States, only 6.5 deaths occurred per 1,000 births. Life expectancy at birth in Botswana was just 33 years of age, while most Americans can expect to live to be 77.

In large part, the reason for these startling differences between Botswana and the United States is the AIDS virus, which has reached epidemic proportions in Botswana. It affects every ethnic and language group in the country, from urban dwellers in Gaborone to those who reside in the smallest desert communities.

Despite the challenges it faces, Botswana boasts high literacy rates (almost 80 percent of Batswana can read and write), a free and open democracy, and a successful economy.

Above: **Wealthy Batswana shop in an upscale mall in Gaborone.**

Opposite: **A mother and her child in Jedibe village, northwest of Maun.**

Two women and a girl carry buckets on their heads in Gaborone. Women do most of the household chores since traditional perceptions of women are still deeply entrenched.

DAILY VILLAGE LIFE

Most of the approximately 50 percent of Batswana who live outside major cities and towns pursue traditional lives that rely on centuries-old customs. Although much homogenization has occurred, differences still exist among the various ethnic groups that make up Botswana society. Traditional Tswana culture and economy centered upon raising cattle, for instance, while traditional !Kung lived as nomadic hunters and gatherers. Although political, social, and economic changes throughout the country have transformed many aspects of traditional life, many Batswana continue to follow age-old customs.

For most Batswana communities, democracy and consultation—called *morero* in Setswana—remain important ideals. The Tswana have an expression that sums up their philosophy: "*Ntwa kgolo ke ya molomo,*" which means "the highest form of war is dialogue." Tolerance of opposing views has long been a part of Botswana culture, which may be one reason why the country remains such a strong and peaceful democracy today.

Another important social custom is sharing. A wealthier Tswana, for instance, will lend a relative who is less well-off some cattle to raise on their own. The cattle loaned out in this way are called *mafisa.* After some time, the owner retrieves the cattle, often leaving several behind as a show of appreciation. The !Kung also share resources found on the land. Groups related by marriage, for instance, may choose to live together in a region where food and water is plentiful, but then willingly separate when resources become scarce. No matter who brings food home to a camp, the food is distributed to everyone living there.

Another Tswana tradition related to sharing is *letsema*, a form of volunteer work by community members on behalf of an individual family or for the benefit of the village at large. A *letsema* may involve anything from plowing village fields to building a neighbor's new home.

THE TSWANA

Traditional Tswana families usually have three homes: one in a village, one built close to their farms, and one at the cattle post. In the villages, many Tswana live in traditional round houses called *rondavels*, which are made of clay and have thatched roofs supported by wooden poles. Others choose to build rectangular homes. Family members usually live in houses close to one another in the villages. At the *masimo*, or "lands," where families spend up to six months per year, Tswana build similar types of homes located near their farmlands. Those families that herd cattle also keep a home at the *moraka*, or cattle post. Usually, only the men stay at the *moraka* while the women stay in the village or at the *masimo*.

Bundles of straw form the frame of the *rondavel*, supported by logs. On this, mud, clay, and sometimes dung are applied to the walls.

Daily life in traditional families continues to revolve around taking care of livestock and growing and preparing food, as it has for centuries. Tswana women are responsible for most of the cooking. They make flour by pounding corn or sorghum in large containers and then turn that flour into porridge using milk or water. They cook over an open fire, usually using wood that they collect from the bush outside the villages.

On a larger scale than the individual village, each group of Tswana forms a *morafe*, or group, each led by a *kgosi*, or chief. Traditionally, the *kgosi* was entrusted with great responsibility over the members of his

75

morafe, including holding all its land in trust and distributing it to those under his authority. The *kgosi* were assisted by counselors and *dikgosana*, or headmen, who helped manage areas away from the main village. Today, the *kgosi* still wield some influence. They hold seats in the House of Chiefs and contribute to the national political agenda.

BUSHMEN SOCIAL ORGANIZATION

For centuries, the Bushmen of Botswana lived nomadic lives in the Kalahari desert and throughout central Botswana. During the past century, more and more Bushmen have integrated into mainstream Botswana society, living more pastoral lives in small villages and towns alongside Tswana and other groups. At least a few thousand remained in the Kalahari until the Botswana government began to relocate them in recent years. The battle for the survival of their ancestral lifestyle continues.

A Bushmen community gather around the rocks of Tsodilo Hills.

Traditionally, the Bushmen formed small communities, called bands, of about 10 to 30 people, usually closely related. Each band lived in its own camp. A camp consisted of about six shelters, made of woven grass supported on sticks, arranged in a half- or quarter-circle around an open plaza. Individuals worked together to hunt and gather food in the area, called the *n!ore*. Sometimes, a resident of one *n!ore* would marry someone from another in order for the communities to more easily share their resources.

When the food and water supplies grew scarce, members of a camp would move together within the *n!ore* to find new resources. Unlike the Tswana and other groups, a Bushmen community is egalitarian, meaning no one person is in charge of governing the camp's activities or controlling land distribution. Because of their minority status, the !Kung do not have representation in the national government.

These Bushmen children enjoy themselves at a camp during the school holidays. Many of them are relocated from their families and ancestral homes by the government to receive education, in a bid for them to fit into modern society.

THE ROLE OF THE FAMILY

As is true for many other countries, the role of the family in Botswana has been influenced by the rapid urbanization and industrialization of the country. The Tswana, the Bushmen, and other groups of Batswana each have their own traditions when it comes to the family and its importance in their cultures.

In the Tswana culture, a family unit is made up of several households that trace their family ties to the same grandfather or great-grandfather. The ancestral lineage of most Tswana family groups can be identified through their *sereto* or totem. A *sereto* is an animal, object, or symbol adopted by each family group. One generation passes this totem to the next generation.

Traditional Tswana families regarded the husband as the absolute head of the family, although attitudes have changed in recent years to offer more equality between husband and wife. This change in the family dynamic, which has occurred in other ethnic groups as well, has taken place largely because more and more wives are employed outside the home and husbands are no longer the sole breadwinners.

A Kalahari !Kung woman and her baby.

When it comes to children and their parents, Batswana expect their children not only to respect their parents but also to provide them with material support as they age. The extended family also is important. Among the Tswana, for instance, maternal uncles are assigned a prominent role in their nephews' and nieces' lives, and cousins also form strong bonds among themselves. In some traditional societies, cousins were

encouraged to marry in order to strengthen family bonds, but the practice is no longer promoted.

Throughout Botswana, grandparents and other elders are among the most loved and respected members of the community. It is not uncommon for parents to arrange for one or more of their children to stay with their grandparents and help with chores. Grandparents serve as conveyors of tradition and history for both the community and the family unit.

A woman and her five children outside their shared house, where they occupy a single room. Although the economy is improving, wealth does not reach all Batswana, and many families have to live in such shared housing.

PASSING DOWN PROPERTY

How property passes from one generation to another differs among the races. Traditionally, Tswana families passed property—mainly cattle—from the deceased to the eldest male member of the family. Younger sons received very little from their fathers, and daughters inherited almost nothing. In addition to receiving property, the eldest son also assumed the responsibility of supporting his mother and other family members. Called *boswa* in Setswana, this system of inheritance is changing today. In most modern Tswana families, the surviving spouse inherits the property and all children, irrespective of gender or age, receive a share of the family possessions. Many Tswana, today, choose to designate their heirs in written wills.

It should be noted that not all Batswana follow the patrilineal system of inheritance, in which males receive and control their families' property. In many other groups, including the Bushmen, women act as heads of households and property passes from the deceased matriarch to the eldest daughter. Every Herero belongs to two clans: the *oruzo*, or partriarchal, line and the *eanda*, or matriarchal line. Traditionally, children inherited residence and religion from their fathers, while property was passed from mother to the eldest daughter.

A Herero mother and child. Property is passed down the matrilineal line in Herero society.

MILESTONES OF LIFE

Although modified by contact with Christian traditions and teachings, customs surrounding the birth of children, puberty, marriage, and death remain integral to traditional Batswana groups.

PREGNANCY AND BIRTH In traditional Tswana culture, infants were thought to come from the *badimo* (bah-DI-moh), ancestral spirits who govern the human world. Today, it is more common for Tswana to view this in Christian terms, with children bestowed by God, called Modimo by Setswana speakers. In either case, the arrival of a new member of the family, and the group, is cause of great joy.

Many groups in Botswana follow traditions surrounding a pregnancy. In both the Tswana and Herero cultures, for instance, pregnant women live separately from their husbands for a period of time. An expectant Herero mother leaves her home shortly after learning of her pregnancy to stay with her mother. A Tswana woman stays confined to her own home with her mother and other female relatives from about six months into her pregnancy until the birth. A Tswana husband stops sharing his wife's room and often leaves the home to stay with male relatives or to travel to another village. A messenger is sent to inform him of the birth. He will wait another several weeks, however, to see the new child.

Following the birth, the traditional young mother and infant remain with female relatives in their village. About three months later, the Tswana celebrate the birth of the child in a ceremony called *Go Ntsha Botsesi*, a naming ceremony accompanied by traditional dancing and feasting.

PUBERTY In the past, when Batswana boys and girls reached puberty, they were expected to enter special schools, called *bogwera* (bog-WER-a)

Although many Batswana choose to deliver their babies in modern hospitals or clinics, many still choose to give birth with the help of traditional midwives. Some traditional midwives have considerable experience and training. Unfortunately, especially in places where emergency medical assistance is scarce, many babies die needlessly at birth. The government continues efforts to improve access to healthcare for all Batswana, such as increasing medical training to traditional midwives.

Today, relatively few Batswana undergo initiation or participate in mephato. *Like many other indigenous traditions, these customs were discouraged by European colonists, who provided schools that offered instruction not only in Christian traditions, but also in English and Western subjects.*

for boys and *bojale* (bog-JAH-le) for girls. Attending these initiation schools marked the passage from childhood to adulthood.

Over a period of about three months, Batswana youth would learn the traditions and customs of their groups from their elders. Boys had to learn how to live in the bush and hunt and kill animals for food. They practiced carpentry, shield-making, and male dances important to group celebrations. At the end of their time at *bogwera*, the boys were circumcised, which was considered the final step from boyhood to manhood. Girls, at *bojale* learned the traditional duties of running the household and raising children. They, too, were considered adults and thus ready for marriage once they completed *bojale*.

For the boys, *bogwera* also formed them into *mephato*, or age regiments. The boys that "graduated" from *bogwera* together formed a *mophato*, a unit of like-aged young men who could be called upon by the community to carry out certain activities ranging from constructing public buildings, forming a militia, or responding to emergencies. The *dikgosi* would give each *mephato* a unique name, usually relating to an event that had taken place during *bogwera*, such as a thunderstorm. In the past, *mephato* were necessary in villages that had no other resource to perform community services. Even today, members of a *mophato* form special bonds with one another that last throughout their lives.

MARRIAGE Traditionally, parents arranged marriages in Botswana. Procreation was the main object of marriage and childbearing was strictly reserved for married couples. In modern Botswana, as elsewhere however, pre-marital sex and single motherhood is common.

Officially, a couple is legally married in Botswana once they have celebrated either civil marriage or customary marriage. Marriage by civil rite

is governed by Roman Dutch law and takes place in a ceremony at a courthouse or a church. Customary marriage takes place in the village and occurs when the parents of the groom and bride make a marriage agreement or *patlo*. Included in the agreement is the payment of *bogadi*, or bride price, usually paid in a number of cattle. Still practiced today in some groups, the payment of *bogadi* was once considered an expression of gratitude by the groom's family to the bride's family for trusting their son to take care of his new bride. More and more Batswana reject the payment of *bogadi* as demeaning to women as well as impractical considering the high rates of divorce. The couple is socially recognized after the *patlo* ceremony takes place; the payment of *bogadi*, if undertaken, may take place at a later date.

Most modern wedding ceremonies in Botswana combine both traditional and Christian practices. Couples may choose to visit a local church to have the marriage blessed and registered with the government, then celebrate with family in either traditional or Western style. Just as is true in the United States, festive receptions usually follow the marriage ceremonies. These are often filled with dancing, singing, and feasting.

For people living
in areas far from
village schools,
the Remote Area
Development
Program (RADP)
provides funds
and other support.
Managed by the
local government,
the RADP may
supply food,
lodging, and
uniforms for
students who move
away from home
to attend school.

DEATH AND MOURNING Among most traditional cultures, death is the time when a person's spirit returns from the world of the living to the world of the dead where they meet their ancestors. Among the Herero, families set aside some cattle to sacrifice at the funerals of loved ones. The cattle accompany the deceased on his or her journey. The Tswana traditionally bury their dead behind the family household. After wrapping the body in cowhide, they place it in the grave in a sitting position to make it easier for the deceased to stand and greet his or her ancestors. Today, villages and towns generally have one common cemetery where everyone is buried after death. The burial is commemorated by either traditional or Christian rituals, or a combination of both.

COPING WITH AN EPIDEMIC

Perhaps nothing has transformed the lifestyle of Batswana more than the deadly AIDS epidemic. In 2001 Botswana's President Festus Mogae put the challenge faced by his country in this stark way, "We are threatened by extinction. People are dying in chillingly high numbers. It is a crisis of the first magnitude." According to recent government statistics, more than 35 percent of the country's adult population is infected with HIV, the virus that causes AIDS. Almost 80,000 Batswana children are now orphans because both of their parents have succumbed to the disease, dramatically changing the children's future prospects. Life expectancy in this country, once approaching Western levels of above 60 years of age, now stands at just 34 years. The AIDS crisis has challenged every aspect of the Botswana way of life, from education to marriage to the numbers of funerals villagers must now attend. And yet Batswana continue to live with hope and vitality, having launched one of the most extensive and successful AIDS prevention and treatment programs in the world.

EDUCATION

Formal education consists of a seven-year primary school program followed by five-year secondary school education. From there students may choose to attend either technical colleges or university.

Primary school students are required to learn subjects such as English, Setswana, mathematics, environmental science, and cultural studies, among others. At the end of the seven-year course is the Primary School Leaving Examination. Secondary school curriculum includes the natural sciences, the humanities, and commerce subjects, and concludes with the General Certificate of Secondary Education.

The University of Botswana is located in Gaborone. Founded in 1964 as the University of Botswana, Lesotho, and Swaziland, it is the country's first institution of higher education and boasts six departments that include business, education, engineering, humanities, science, and social sciences, and an increasing number of graduate programs. Its motto is *Thuto Ke Thebe*, which means "education is a shield" in Setswana.

About 16,000 full-time and part-time students attend the University of Botswana every year, studying under about 800 teaching staff.

RELIGION

EXCEPT WITH HIS OWN CONSENT, no person shall be hindered in the enjoyment of his freedom of conscience, and for the purposes of this section, the said freedom includes freedom of thought and religion, freedom to change his religion or belief, and freedom, either alone or in community with others, and both public and private, to manifest and propagate his religion or belief in worship, teaching, practice, and observance.

With these words, Botswana's constitution provides its people with the freedom to observe and practice any religion. Since European Christian missionaries first arrived in the 19th century, more and more Batswana have chosen to worship within the Christian tradition. In fact, all eight Tswana states adopted Christianity as their official religion. However, traditional African religions continue to survive in most Botswana communities, practiced in their complete form or partially incorporated into the practice of other faiths.

Although these religions differ in certain respects, most have common traditions and beliefs, including the central tenets of sharing, communal living, and what the Tswana term *botho*. *Botho* refers to attributes a person needs if he or she wants to be considered a good human being. Good-manners, compassion, humility, and respect for others and for society in general are among the qualities required to have *botho*. In addition, most traditional faiths share core beliefs in a supreme creator and lesser divine beings that watch over humankind from above.

Above: **This woman, a traditional healer, places the tools of her craft, on the ground as a man consults her for advice.**

Oppposite: **A priest of the Zion Christian Church leads his congregation in the singing of hymns.**

THE SUPREME BEING

All of the traditional religions in Botswana believe in a single great being that created the world and provided the people with everything they needed to live. Each group has a different name for this being, but most portray him as masculine and as benevolent.

In the traditional Tswana religion, most groups refer to their supreme being as Modimo. Modimo is responsible not only for the creation of humankind, but also of animal and plants, which explains in part the deep spiritual connection between the Tswana and their natural environment. The !Kung have many names for the great God who created all the earth and all that is in it, including !Xu, or N!dima. !Xu has a wife called Koba, which means "mother of the bees." The Herero have yet other names for the creator, including Omukuru and Njambi Karunga.

In most Batswana traditions, the creator remains unseen. He lives in the heavens and rarely acts directly upon the earth, but instead works his will through lesser gods who are the spirits of the people's ancestors.

THE STORY OF CREATION

Each major group has its own story that describes how the earth was created. Traditional Tswana, for example, believed that they all came from a common ancestor named Matsieng, who emerged through a hole in the ground from the underworld, leaving his footprints in the still-new landscape. He also brought goats, sheep, and cattle with him to sustain the people. Ancient footprints found at a site about 25 miles (15 km) from the capital city of Gaborone are believed by Tswana to be those of Matsieng. The hole from which he emerged is about 6 feet (4 m) deep and filled with water.

The name "Modimo" is thought to be sacred and believers avoid invoking it for fear of offending the supreme god.

Bushman rock paintings on rocks in Tsodilo Hills.

For most of the Bushmen groups, the Tsodilo Hills were the site of creation. They believe that !Xu lowered them, and livestock to feed them, to the earth from this spot. Their supporting evidence consists of hoof and foot prints clearly etched into a rock high on one of the hills. Along with !Xu, the !Kung honor several lesser deities, including G!aoan, who sends messages to human beings by way of their ancestors.

SPIRITS

Traditional Batswana groups believe deeply in a spirit world, parallel to our own. Two types of spirits exist: the spirits of family members who have died and other spirits, who are either good or evil. All spirits can act as intermediaries between people and the supreme creator.

Ancestral worship is central to most traditional Batswana religions. These ancestral spirits are not only guardians of all living things, but they may also affect natural occurrences, such as the onset of rains and the harvest. In return for their protection, the living perform certain rituals and ceremonies on behalf of these spirits.

The Tswana call their ancestral spirits *badimo*. Before drinking or eating meals on important occasions, people are supposed to place some drink or food on the ground to feed the *badimo*. The Herero, who call their ancestor spirits *ovakuru*, must keep a sacred fire burning in their village in order to maintain good relationships with the spirits. If the people fail to follow these rituals, the offended spirits can cause illness or other misfortunes to befall one or more members of the group.

COMMUNICATING WITH SPIRITS

In order to communicate with the spirit world, traditional Batswana usually go through diviners and healers, members of their groups whom they believe hold special powers. Diviners are believed to be able to look into the spirit world in order to locate the spirit responsible for an individual's or group's misfortune. They may also be able to see the future. According to traditional Tswana beliefs, a diviner can intervene when a *boloi* (bo-LOY) or witch, casts an evil spell on one of the group. Tswana diviners can diagnose illnesses and then treat them with herbs either alone or with the help of a traditional healer. The healer usually has an extensive knowledge of Botswana's wide range of medicinal herbs and plants.

According to traditional beliefs, offending the spirit world could directly affect the natural world. Traditional Tswana, for instance, believe that a failure to respect the *badimo* causes drought, which is a frequent occurrence in Botswana's semi-arid climate. The responsibility for appeasing the *badimo* during times of drought falls upon the *kgosi*, or leader of the group. Each Tswana group has its own particular rainmaking ceremony, but most center on the sacrifice of one or more cows. After the sacrifice, the *kgosi* mixes the cow's blood with herbs, takes it to a sacred place, and uses a branch to sprinkle the mixture throughout the area.

HEALING THE !KUNG WAY

In the Bushmen tradition, performing all-night healing dances is the main method for treating illnesses. In a healing dance, everyone shares a deep spiritual power, called *n!om*, which the Bushmen believe resides in the fire that burns in their midst and in the songs that they sing. During the dance, the healers in the group begin to activate this energy and may fall into a trance, or heightened state of awareness, known as *!aia*. When the state of *!aia* occurs, a healer's powers to treat disease is particularly potent.

Not only can a healing dance cure illnesses, but it can help solve domestic and social disputes and appease angry spirits. Healing in the Bushmen culture also means adding to each person's emotional and spiritual growth. Most traditional Bushmen groups hold healing dances about three times a month.

THE EARLY MISSIONARIES

During the 19th century, a movement to convert the world to Christianity emerged from Europe. Africa became a chosen destination for young missionaries who sought to educate Africans about the Christian faith.

Two of the most important missionaries in Botswana's history were Robert Moffat, the first missionary to settle among the Tswana, and David Livingstone *(right)*, his son-in-law and one of Britain's most illustrious explorers. In about 1818 Moffat settled among the Tlhaping group and began to transcribe, or write down, the Tswana language, which had no written script of its own. He also was on hand to help the Tlhaping fight a large army of refugees from the south who had attacked them.

David Livingstone arrived in the region in 1843 and lived among the Kwena group near present-day Molepolole. He baptized one of the most powerful Tswana kings of the region, Sechele, who ruled the Kwena from 1829 to 1892, and helped Sechele in the group's struggle against the Afrikaners. Livingstone also surveyed the Kalahari and discovered Lake Ngami, which sits on the northern edge of the desert, in 1879. He described Ngami as a "shimmering lake, some 80 miles (128 km) long and 20 miles (32 km) wide." As his father-in-law had done with the Tlhaping, Livingstone acted as an intermediary between the Kwena, their neighboring groups, and the increasing numbers of Europeans.

Many Batswana were both grateful for the help provided by the missionaries and were also genuinely interested in the Christian faith. However, today critics believe that many missionaries tended to be insensitive, if not hostile, to local traditions and culture.

CHRISTIANITY

The majority of Batswana are Christians. European missionaries brought Christianity to Botswana in the 19th century. Although Batswana had little trouble assimilating their own beliefs with those set forth by the Christians, the missionaries had conflicts with traditional practices, such as polygamy. In most traditional Batswana societies, men were encouraged to take more than one wife. Despite such differences, most Batswana, particularly the Tswana groups, readily adopted Christian tenets into their traditions, often finding a comfortable blend between the two.

There are three primary types of Christian churches in Botswana today: mission, Pentecostal, and African independent. The mission churches began with the arrival of missionaries in the 19th century. Pentecostal faiths were brought to Botswana sometime later by missionaries from the United States who believed that they had been "born again" to experience the holy spirit. African independent churches emerged as a reaction against the imposition of these churches on traditional Batswana religions.

Today, many, if not most, Batswana Christians have broken away from Western Christianity to set up their own churches which are more sympathetic to African indigenous beliefs or customs. Two of the most popular independent churches are the Zion Christian Church and the Healing Church of Botswana.

OTHER RELIGIONS

Less than 1 percent of Batswana belong to the Muslim faith. Most Batswana Muslims live in Gaborone. A small number of Jews also call Botswana home. Thanks to both the constitutional guarantee of freedom of religion and the Batswana tradition of tolerance and *botho*, people of all faiths continue to feel welcome in this country.

Of the 79 percent of Batswana who identify themselves as Christian, about 30 percent identify themselves as "independent," almost 14 percent "unaffiliated," 11 percent Protestant, and about 4 percent Roman Catholic.

LANGUAGE

ENGLISH IS THE OFFICIAL LANGUAGE of Botswana. Every child who goes to public school learns English from the fifth year of elementary school onward. However, English remains the language of the educated and only about 40 to 50 percent speak and read it fluently. There is very little exposure to English in rural areas and smaller villages.

More than 30 other languages are spoken in Botswana. The most common language is Setswana, a Bantu language in the Sotho-Tswana group. Today, 90 percent of Batswana understand and use Setswana. Many Batswana have called for Setswana to be elevated to an official language, so that the government would have to publish and broadcast all its material in both English and Setswana.

Some Batswana, such as the Kalanga, speak at least three languages: English, Setswana, and their mother tongue. On the other hand, many of those who live in more isolated communities, such as the Bushmen, may speak their own language exclusively. Part of the political debate over minority rights includes how the historical focus on Setswana and English by both colonists and the modern government has contributed to the isolation of smaller groups in Botswana.

SETSWANA

Setswana is a member of the Sotho subgroup of closely-related Bantu languages, which are themselves members of a very large language family that stretches across central, eastern, and southern Africa. The name Bantu comes from the Bantu word for "people." In Setswana, the word for "people" is *batho*. In fact, the Tswana tradition is to place the prefix *ba*, meaning people, before the names of ethnic groups. Thus Tswana become *BaTswana*, the Kalanga becomes *BaKalanga*, and so forth.

Opposite: **A man uses a mobile phone in rural Botswana. Technology is not only changing the way Batswana communicate but also the vocabulary of the native languages spoken in the country.**

Setswana is also spoken as a native language in South Africa, Namibia, and Zimbabwe.

NUMBERS IN SETSWANA

1 *Nngwe* (ing-we)   4 *Nne* (neh)   7 *Supa* (soop-ah)
2 *Pedi* (pe-dee)   5 *Tlhano* (te-oh)   8 *Robedi* (rob-eddy)
3 *Tharo* (tha-row)   6 *Thataro* (at-are-oh)   9 *Robongwe* (rob-eng-wey)
                                                  10 *Lesome* (less-ome)

PRONOUCIATION GUIDE

a — as *a* in "father"   ng — as *ny* in "Netanyahu"
b — as *b* in "bat"   o — as *o* in "order"
d — like *d* in "do"   p — as *p* in "pull"
e — as *e* in "exit"   r — as *r* in "rope" (a rolled *r*)
f — as *f* in "farm"   s — as *s* in "say"
g — as *ch* in "loch"   š — as *tion* in "station"
h — as *h* in "ham"   šw — as *sw* in "swift"
i — as *ea* in "eat"   t — as *t* in "pot"
j — as *j* in "job"   tšh — as *ch* in "church"
k — as *c* in "clerical"   u — as *oo* in "book"
l — as *l* in "list"   w — as *w* in "well"
m — as *m* in "mum"   y — as *y* in "yearn"
n — as *n* in "now"

In Botswana, Setswana is spoken by about 1 million people. Although Setswana has several different dialects, Batswana from different regions can communicate with ease because the dialects are closely related. In fact, experts believe that the word "Batswana" originally came from the term *Ba a tswana*, which means people coming from the same place or people coming from each other. Another possible origin of "Batswana" is *Ba a tshwana*, which means "they are the same."

Internationally, there are about 4 million Setswana speakers. The largest number of speakers reside in South Africa, where about 3 million people, or 8 percent, of the South African population speak the language. In fact, Setswana is one of South Africa's official languages. In Botswana, two newspapers, the daily *Dikgang Tsa Gompieno* and the monthly *Kutlwana*, are published in Setswana. Most Batswana speak one of four dialects of Setswana: Ngwaketse, Ngwato, Kwena, and Kgatla. The Kgatla dialect is the one used by the educational and economic elite of the country, though all of the dialects are very similar.

A CULTURAL MIX OF LANGUAGES

Linguists studying the evolution of Setswana in Botswana and elsewhere have noted that a new version of the language is making itself heard. Over the years, Setswana speakers in Botswana have borrowed many words from other languages, particularly English. Younger Batswana, more exposed to Western television and movies than their parents, are particularly vulnerable to speaking the "new" language.

Even large corporations are using this mixture of English and Setswana to advertise their products. Mascom, for instance, the country's market leader in mobile communications, dubbed one of its products "Nzamela airtime," using the Setswana place name and the English word for the service it offers. This new jargon is especially common when it comes to terms connected with computers and the Internet. The Setswana word for "e-mail," for instance, is *e-maili* and the word "computer" in Setswana is *khomputa* (com-pute-ah).

At the same time, many Setswana words are used by English-speaking Batswana, including terms like *kglota*, which is a traditional community meeting place, and *matimela*, which are stray cattle.

Batswana women attend a basic literacy class in Gabarone. With support from the government, the literacy rate rose to 78.9 percent in 2003.

97

A classroom for !Kung San children near the Kalahari. Batswana are taught both Setswana and English in school. English, however, is the only official language in the country.

WRITING IT DOWN

Setswana was the first Sotho language to have a written form. After missionary Dr. Robert Moffat arrived to live among the Tlhaping in 1818, he built the first school for the people of Botswana. In 1825 he realized that he needed to speak and write Setswana in order to teach his pupils and began the long process of writing down the language. The first works he translated from English into Setswana were religious texts, specifically *The Gospel According to Luke*, the *New Testament*, and the *Old Testament*.

The first Motswana who contributed to the history of written Setswana is Solomon T. Plaatje. A Setswana speaker born in South Africa, Plaatje authored the first novel in English by a black African. His book, *Mhudi: An Epic of South African Native Life One Hundred Years Ago*, was published in 1930. Plaatje moved to Mafeking, the capital of the British protectorate Bechuanaland as a court reporter shortly before the South African War. During the Siege of Mafeking (1899–1900), he kept a journal, *The Boer War Diary of Sol T. Plaatje*, which was published in 1973, after his death. He also translated a number of English works into Setswana, including many of those of William Shakespeare.

WORDS AND EXPRESSIONS

Setswana, as well as other Bantu languages, uses prefixes to indicate singular and plural nouns. Bantu noun classes relate to conceptual categories. Thus kinship terms tend to belong to one noun class, inanimate objects to another, and abstract concepts to yet another. Noun classes are indicated by prefixes added to a noun stem. Sometimes with proper nouns the stem is written with a capital initial to clarify the construction. *BaTswana*, therefore, would mean "members of the Tswana group."

Someone visiting Botswana is likely to learn the word *dumela* (DOO-mella), which means "hello." When speaking to a man, it is polite to address him as *rra* (rah), which means "sir" and to address a woman as *mma* (mah), which means "madam."

BUSHMEN

The Bushmen of Botswana speak one of the languages in the Khoisan group. The name Khoisan comes from the name of the Khoi-Khoi group of South Africa and the !Kung group of Namibia and Botswana. Bantu groups who migrated south and European colonists who arrived later used the term San to identify the original inhabitants of Botswana.

The formal way to enquire about someone's health is "O tsogile jang?" the literal translation of which is "How did you awake?" A casual way of asking how someone is feeling is "Le kae?" (Lay kye) or "How are you?"

The Khoisan language family is the smallest of the language families in Africa. Several are known to have become extinct. Today, only about 13 Khoisan languages have more than 1,000 speakers. In Botswana, most Bushmen (about 14,000) speak Naro, although several other Khoisan languages are present. Some Bushmen in Botswana, primarily those who work on farms and in cities, also speak Setswana and English.

SPEAKING !KUNG

All members of this unique family of languages share some similarities in their extremely complex sound systems. Vowels are spoken with the use of several vocal features, including nasalization (the production of sound so that air escapes partially or wholly through the nose), pharyngealization (an articulation of the sound by pressing the back of the tongue into the throat), and other different voice qualities such as a breathy or a creaking voice.

Consonants are pronounced using up to five basic click sounds. The exclamation point in the written form of the language represents one of the click sounds. There are three main types of clicks: dental, alveolar, and lateral. A dental click sounds like "tsk, tsk!" and is made by putting the tongue just behind the front teeth. An alveolar click sounds like a popping cork and is made by putting the tongue just behind the ridge in back of the front teeth. An alveo-palatal click is a sharp pop made by drawing the tongue down quickly from the roof of the mouth. A lateral click sounds like the "che-che" sound used in English to urge on a horse. A bi-labial click is a pop made by bringing the lips together and releasing, making a sound just like a kiss. Each click can be accompanied by other

A !Kung San child practices her reading.

The Bokamoso Trust is an independent, non-governmental organization that aims to enable children from different minorities, including the Bushmen, to have access to early childhood education provided in a culturally sensitive manner. The Trust is part of a broader group of organizations called the Kuru Family of Organizations that are run by the Bushmen. The Trust seeks to promote self-esteem and build self-confidence among the people it works with by teaching them their mother tongues, including Naro in Botswana. In Botswana the Bokamoso Trust has worked in 14 communities with a combined population of about 20,000 people since about 1988.

Working with the Trust are two Dutch linguists, Hessel and Coby Visser. Until recently, Naro was an unwritten language. Thanks to the Vissers, however, there is now a Naro-English dictionary as well as several English texts translated into Naro. Every year, the Vissers travel to each school involved in the Bokamoso project and help train teachers in the Naro language.

vocal features, including nasalization and aspiration, which is a strong burst of air following the sound of the click.

The word and sentence structure of the various Khoisan languages differ considerably. However, most Khoisan nouns fall into three groups, based on gender: masculine, feminine, and common. A grammatical feature common to many Khoisan languages is the use of verb compounds. Where English would use a single verb, such as "enter," a Bushman would use two or more verbs, such as "go/enter." The vocabulary of the !Kung is a reflection of their lifestyles. They have a very complex word list related to hunting, animals, plants, and various types of terrain.

INDIGENOUS LANGUAGES

There are a large number of languages spoken in Botswana by various ethnic groups, some by as few as 800 people. More than 150,000 Batswana speak Kalanga, another Bantu language. Kalanga speakers generally live in the country's Northeast District. About 40,000 Kgalagadi speakers live mostly along the border with South Africa and in the western half of the country's Southern District. About 20,000 people in Botswana speak Herero, which is part of the Bantu family of languages. Also known as Otjiherero, it has several different dialects, including Herero, Mbanderu, and Chimba. Herero speakers live throughout the country, usually inhabiting their own ethnic enclaves within larger towns and villages.

ARTS

BOTSWANA'S MUSIC, literature, and arts and crafts mirror the country's rich cultural diversity. Every ethnic group has contributed to a flourishing arts community that focuses not just on the past but also on Botswana's present and future.

MUSICAL TRADITIONS

Singing, dancing, and playing musical instruments are all favorite pastimes of modern Batswana. Traditional Tswana music is known for its focus on the human voice and stringed instruments. Musical instruments include the *sebaga* (se-BAY-ga), a unique one-stringed instrument from which experienced musicians are able to elicit a multitude of notes. As one Botswana arts magazine described it, the *sebaga* "produces music that combines the twanging of the arrow released from the strings with the sound made by tapping the strings with a stick." Another instrument is the *setinkana*, which consists of tongues of metal of different lengths mounted on a wooden board set inside a gourd or calabash. Shells, bottle tops, or rings are attached to the soundboard. When the strings are plucked, they make a characteristic buzzing sound. *Setinkana* music is cyclical in nature, which means it is played continuously from beginning to end. Its meter is precise, like the ticking of a clock, and must flow in an unbroken stream.

Children are taught traditional music and dance at school. Many schools hold traditional dance competitions every year where children from all over the region show off their talents. The dancers wear beaded

Above: **This !Kung woman plays a thumb piano by striking metal keys of varying lengths attached to a wooden base.**

Opposite: **A woman weaves a traditional basket using strips of palm fronds.**

103

Bushmen perform a traditional dance in Gaborone.

As well as focusing on modern music, Batswana have incorporated their traditional music into church singing, and gospel choirs are now among the most popular groups in the country.

jewelry and costumes made of skins. A popular traditional Tswana dance is the *setapa*, which is performed by youths as they return from initiation schools.

The Bushmen also have a strong musical heritage. Their haunting music has been recorded and sold to international audiences. The instruments include tools they use to survive in the desert, such as bows and digging sticks. Other !Kung instruments are the rattle, made from the fruit of the green monkey tree, and the *quasi*, a stringed instrument made from a hollowed tree with a strings fixed across it.

Since independence, popular music has been largely dominated by South African and African-American artists. According to a 2002 story in Botswana's *Daily News*, it was not until the 1980s, when Botswana artists such as Afro-Sunshine and Duncan Senyatso recorded their first albums, that the local music industry came to life. Even then, lack of knowledge about the music industry held back many local artists. Today, however, there appears to be a burgeoning Botswana music scene.

MY AFRICAN DREAM

On October 7, 2005, more than 2,000 young Batswana came together at the Gaborone International Convention Center for the 10th annual "My African Dream" talent competition. The aim of the non-profit event is to target Batswana youth interested in the performing arts and offer them an opportunity to perform in front of their peers. With the backing of more than 30 schools in Gaborone that run local talent competitions, young Batswana are encouraged to master a wide range of performance skills, especially dancing and singing. In 2001 government-run Botswana television agreed to both host the show and broadcast the event each year.

The show's tenth anniversary showcased the talents of two groups of *kwaito* (KWAY-toh) dancers, the Weather Girls and Stemrico, who won in the senior and junior categories of the competition. Similar to hip hop in the United States, *kwaito* is the music of young, black, urban southern Africans. It is a mixture of modern music young people all over the world listen to: hip hop, reggae, and American and British house music. It has its roots in the South African city of Johannesburg, where most of the population is black, poor, and recovering from the repressive days of apartheid. And it's not just music: *Kwaito* is also a style of dress, of language, and of dancing.

BOTSWANA LITERATURE

Until relatively recently, Batswana had no written language. However, they fostered a great oral tradition of storytelling and poetry that passed on their history and culture as well as entertained. Today, several Batswana authors are well-respected in their own country and around the world.

As is true for many American families, a favorite source of entertainment and learning is storytelling by grandparents to their grandchildren. Called *mainane*, the folktales told by one generation to the next help entertain children as well as impart moral lessons. Like fairytales in the West, *mainane* often feature mythical creatures and magical animals as their main characters. The Bushmen, too, have a rich tradition of storytelling. One of their favorite creatures is the praying mantis who can turn into any animal. In one tale, the praying mantis becomes a hartebeest, a type of antelope. Even after it is killed by children who find it, it is able to put itself back together and chase after the terrified children.

Proverbs are also an important form of Batswana language arts. Short, snappy phrases encapsulate lessons in morality: To indicate living life in the lap of luxury, a Tswana might utter *"A Hura ja Mmotlana, boroko!"*, which means "O sleep the poor man's fat!" A popular proverb for those who might consider celebrating another person's misfortune is *O se tshege yo o oleng, mareledi a sale pele,* or "Do not laugh at someone who has fallen. There are slippery slopes ahead."

The first Motswana to publish a novel outside of the country is Unity Dow. Her first novel, *Far and Beyon'*, describes a family in a rural village in modern-day Botswana struggling to come to terms with the contradictions between traditional and western values, gender conflicts, and the crisis of the AIDS epidemic. Unity Dow also claims another Botswana first. A human rights activist and lawyer, Dow was appointed as the country's first female judge on the High Court in January 1998.

BASKETRY AND OTHER CRAFTS

Although mass-produced items tend to dominate homes of most modern Batswana, traditional crafts, such as basket weaving, pottery, and woodcarving remain important to the artists who create them, as well as to tourists who especially enjoy these tangible reflections of a country's culture.

A simple basket to hold grain or transport food becomes a beautiful work of art in the hands of Batswana basket weavers, who are among the finest in Africa. Usually made by wrapping the leaves of the mokolwane palm around grass straws, the colorful baskets showcase designs—often representing animals and nature—that have been passed from generation to generation.

The primary tool used in basket weaving is the *lemao* (lem-MAO), a sharp piece of thick wire set in a wooden handle. Weavers pierce the tight coils with the *lemao*, which allows them to insert and wrap the palms around the straws. Roots and barks are entwined to create the basket's colored patterns. Since 1973, when the Botswanacraft Marketing Company started to market Botswana baskets outside of the country, more and more people from around the world have come to appreciate the craft.

There are several potteries in Botswana that produce unusual and creative pottery. Dinkgwana pottery, located outside of Lobatse, uses gray clay from the local river. Potters mold the clay by first forming coils then gradually building the pot from its base. Gabane pottery located just outside Gaborone, on the other hand, is known for its rich glazes in traditional African colors.

A weaver at work at a co-operative in Odi, a crafts village located northeast of Gaborone. The crafts here are well known for their bright and modern designs.

The prevalence of a wide variety of trees has made woodcarving popular among Batswana artisans. *Morala*, a yellowish hardwood, is used for spoons and bowls; *mokomoto*, a white wood, is often chosen to make carvings of animals and toys, and *morula*, also of a whitish color, is used mainly for the carving of traditional bowls. Black designs, made by burning the surface with hot pieces of metal, often appear on the lighter woods. Carvings of animals and birds dominate the craft, although some wood carvers still create household items, such as the traditional *kika*, or mortar, and *motshe*, pestle.

Herero women are accomplished seamstresses who make colorful patchwork dresses out of fine cloth. They are also known for the dolls they make, complete with clothing that represents every stage of a woman's life from childhood to old age. The !Kung are also known for their skills with needle and thread. They create clothing and accessories such as hats and handbags out of leather and other animal skins. They also fashion beads out of stone, glass, and ostrich eggs, hand-drilling each one which they use to create beaded handbags, aprons, and bracelets.

A Basarwa woman sings in appreciation as she receives a gift of necklaces.

EXPRESSION THROUGH PAINTING

Traditional painting among Batswana is practically as old as the land itself. The !Kung rock paintings in the Tsolido Hills date back several centuries, and Tswana decorations on the walls of traditional homes have been passed down through generations. Called *lekgapho* (lek-GAP-ho) these murals etched into the mud walls depict a wide variety of scenes, from animals to more abstract designs. As Botswana continues to modernize, and more concrete homes are built, this art may slowly die out.

When it comes to modern art, the National Museum & Art Gallery in Gaborone is the centerpiece for Botswana. Opened in 1968, it now holds regular exhibitions of local artists. Every April it hosts the annual "Artists in Botswana," which draws hundreds of visitors to see paintings and crafts created by artists from all over the country. A leading modern Tswana painter is Phillip Segola, who also acts as the museum's curator. Three female artists, Coex'ae Qgam, Ann Gollifer, and Neo Matome, often exhibit their paintings together. Although they are all from Botswana, each offers a different style, from traditional to contemporary.

A modern Bushmen painter of renown is Thamae Setshogo. After growing up on the edge of the Central Kalahari Game Reserve, Thamae now creates colorful oil paintings on canvas. He is also an expert printmaker, famous for his large black and white prints. In 1997 Thamae received a commission to make a large relief wall panel for the Princess Marina Hospital in Gaborone. During the same year, he painted a large mural for the "Return of the Moon" exhibition held at the National Museum in Windhoek, Namibia.

The National Museum & Art Gallery in Gaborone houses many important pieces of art by prominent Batswana artists.

LEISURE

FOR BOTSWANA'S traditional hunters and gatherers, leisure time has been relatively rare. Finding enough food, preparing meals for the day, and preserving and storing supplies for the future are time- and energy-intensive activities. Nevertheless, families and neighborhoods in towns and villages across the land continue to gather together to sing and dance, weave baskets and create other crafts, and play games. As Botswana has modernized, the people in larger cities and towns like Gaborone and Francistown spend their leisure time doing what others around the world tend to do: watch television, surf the Internet, and go to the movies. They also dance at clubs and listen to music. Organized sports are also very popular for both participants and fans alike.

Above: **A youth taking a dip in the Okavango River.**

Opposite: **An international company holds a friendly volleyball tournament for its staff.**

TRADITIONAL VILLAGE GAMES

Perhaps because an important tenet of Botswana's religious traditions is sharing, Batswana love to come together to tell stories and play games and music. Typically, games would involve using toys made from things found in the environment. Both the !Kung and Tswana children play traditional games using melons, the !Kung in a celebratory dance and the Tswana in a game of catch involving singing and dancing. Favorite games of boys and men include throwing a smooth, pliable branch that rebounds once it hits the ground, and flipping up and down a short reed with a weight at one end and a feather at the other.

Mmele is a traditional board game played throughout southern Africa. Similar to chess, it is played between two players, each of whom put 12 pieces down on the board one at a time. Once all the pieces have been

Above: **A tourist plays a game of *mmele* on the sand with a local safari guide.**

Opposite: **A group of youths play an exciting game of basketball. Western sports such as basketball and volleyball are gaining popularity in the country.**

placed, the players move them from one square to the other. Whenever one player gets three of his or her pieces in a row, the player can take one piece from the opponent. The player left with only two pieces loses.

Another traditional game of hide and seek uses the *sebaga*, a one-stringed instrument. According to TswanaMyzer Matlhaku, one of Botswana's leading artists, "the *segaba* player would hide an object, then help his playmates find it by playing more or less elaborate tunes on his instrument to direct the seeker to the object."

SPORTS IN BOTSWANA

As is true for many developing countries, creating a strong sports program that includes professional teams is often very difficult. Although primary and secondary schools, as well as the University of Botswana, offer sports programs to the community, Botswana has not yet raised a winning flag at any international competition.

Botswana competed as an independent country for the first time in the 1980 Olympic Games in Moscow. Despite a demand by the United States for all African countries to boycott the games after the Soviet Union invaded Afghanistan, Botswana felt obligated to participate due to its ties with the Soviet Union, which had provided technical assistance to its sports development program since independence. Botswana also has close ties with Cuba, which provides coaches to train Batswana athletes in track and field and boxing.

Today, Botswana's Department of Sport and Recreation (DSR) coordinates and provides overall leadership for sports development. Its goal is to create an environment in which all Batswana, rural or urban, can participate in sports either for fun, fitness, or recreation. It also intends to provide athletes with the potential to excel with the facilities they need to do so.

Working closely with the DSR, the Botswana National Sports Conference (BNSC) allocates funds to sports organizations throughout the country. The BNSC deals directly with the various sports associations and serves as an intermediary between the government and the national sports associations. The BNSC is made up of representatives of all of the sports organizations in Botswana.

SOCCER: A NATIONAL PASSION

By far, football—the game known as soccer in the United States—is Botswana's favorite sport. Its national team, the Zebras, recently surprised sports fans by advancing further than ever through the Federation International Football Association (FIFA) qualifying rounds for its 2006 World Cup *(below)*. Although they finally lost to Morocco, who beat them 3–1 on September 3, 2005, their fine showing encouraged Batswana eager to see their team compete at an international level.

The star of Botswana's team is 26-year-old Diphetego Selolwane, known simply as "Dipsy" to his fans. Selolwane learned some of his soccer finesse on U.S. soil when he played for the Chicago team, the Chicago Fire, while attending college in Illinois. Equally important to the Zebras' future is its coach, Vesselin Jelusic, who, during his two-and-a-half-year tenure, has taken the country's team further than anyone previously imagined. The Belgrade-born Jelusic has been coaching in Africa since 1992 and is a former coach for the Angolan national team.

OTHER SPORTS

Track and field is another favorite Botswana sport and Amantle Montsho is one of its international stars. The first woman from Botswana to compete in the Olympics when she ran the 400-meter race in 2004, Montsho was named Sportswoman of the Year in 2005.

Boxers from Botswana also have achieved some success at international competitions such as the Olympic Games, the Commonwealth Games, and the All-Africa Games. Although winning medals at the Olympics remains elusive, Batswana boxers won bronze medals at the All-Africa Games in Egypt in 1991 and Zimbabwe in 1995. Boxing, as with other sports, is hampered by a severe lack of funds that restricts the ability of boxers from Botswana to compete in international competitions. For instance, Botswana could only afford to send five boxers instead of an allocated 10 to the Olympic qualifying tournament in Casablanca, Morocco in 2004.

Lechedzani Luza from Botswana, in blue, takes a powerful swipe at his Moroccan opponent in the 2004 Olympic Games held in Athens, Greece.

FESTIVALS

BATSWANA CELEBRATE several public holidays every year. Holidays are either religious occasions or anniversaries of important dates in the country's history, such as Independence Day and the Birthday of Sir Seretse Khama, its first president. The streets of the larger cities, such as Gaborone and Francistown come alive with parades, open air concerts, and vendors selling local delicacies on these days.

Traditional Batswana also commemorate initiations, weddings, and other rites of passage with specific rituals. However, since their first contact with Christian missionaries in the 19th century, many traditional customs have changed to include Western symbols and practices.

Above and opposite: **Holiday celebrations in Botswana sometimes include traditional dance performances.**

NATIONAL HOLIDAYS

Batswana celebrate their holidays as most other people do the world over: listen and play music, dance, and enjoy feasts with family and friends. Decorating homes and villages by painting walls and building facades is also common, as is dressing up in clothes made with hand-dyed fabrics.

For its first three decades, most President's Day celebrations took place in the capital city of Gaborone. When President Festus Mogae succeeded Quett Masire in 1998, however, he took President's Day to the people. Different communities now host the celebrations on a rotating basis. In 2005 the Chobe District was the venue for the country's festivities, which included a folk concert and a soccer tournament. President Mogae also spoke to citizens from Chobe in a speech broadcast to the nation.

An appreciative audience looks on as a military parade is conducted to commemorate the country's independence at the National Stadium in Gaborone.

Another president, Sir Sereste Khama, is recognized by Batswana not only on President's Day but also on the anniversary of his birthday on July 1. Another important public holiday in Botswana is Independence Day. In an article in the government newspaper, *The Daily News*, seventy-year-old Sethoko Sechele described Botswana's first Independence Day in 1966 when the British Union Jack was lowered and replaced by the black, white, and blue striped flag of the new republic. In villages across the country, Batswana decorated their homes with different colors, and poets, musicians, and choirs performed in arenas and *kglota*. As citizens walked through the streets, their friends and neighbors offered them food in celebration.

Although Independence Day remains a national holiday, activities surrounding the holiday largely take place in the capital city of Gaborone. The president marks the day by giving a speech in which he reviews the achievements of the prior year and sets goals for the next. He also gives out awards to citizens and government officials who have contributed to the development and welfare of the country.

RELIGIOUS HOLIDAYS

In Botswana, only Christian holidays are recognized public holidays. These holidays include Christmas Day, Good Friday, Easter Monday, and Ascension Day. As is true for Christians in other countries, the two most important holidays for Christians in Botswana are Christmas and Easter. At Christmas, families first go to church, then come together for dinner. Families and friends also exchange gifts.

Both Good Friday and Easter Monday provide Batswana with three-day weekends in which to celebrate these sacred days. Events include egg rolling competitions and dousing other people with water which, at one time, was holy water used to bless the house and food. Forty days after Easter, Christian Batswana celebrate Ascension Day when, according to the bible, Christ ascended to heaven.

Like followers of Christianity worldwide, Batswana Christians mark Easter and Christmas by attending mass.

OTHER CELEBRATIONS

For nine days each April, the capital city of Gaborone plays host to the country's largest performing arts festival. Complete with street vendors selling traditional delicacies to eat and drink, the annual Maitisong Festival is a great showcase for both established and up-and-coming local talent who perform in many different city venues. *Maitisong* is the Setswana word for traditional.

The festival features two main programs: a free outdoor component staged at four arenas around the capital, and an indoor program, which takes place at various venues around Gaborone, including the Little Theatre at the National Museum and the Anglican Church. The indoor events charge admission fees.

WORLD PRESS FREEDOM DAY

Since 1991, journalists throughout the world observe World Press Freedom Day on May 3. The idea for the holiday was conceived by a group of African publishers and journalists gathered at a UNESCO conference in Windhoek, Namibia. They wanted to encourage and develop ideas that would foster a free press, as well as to assess the state of press freedom worldwide. In Botswana, journalists often mark the day with marches in favor of decreased censorship, which has manifested itself in the cancellation of a political column published in the country's most read newspaper by Botswana's Communication Ministry, and increased attention to professional ethics among reporters, editors, and publishers.

WORLD AIDS DAY

With one of the highest rates of HIV and AIDS infection in the world, Botswana takes every opportunity to educate its citizens on its extensive prevention and treatment programs. World AIDS Day, which falls on December 1, helps them to do just that.

In 2005 the theme of World AIDS Day in Botswana was "Women, Girls, HIV/AIDS." In the 15 to 19 age group, HIV prevalence was 12 times higher in girls than in boys and, in pregnant women, HIV rates were as high as 39 percent. Dr. Peter Piot, the executive director of the United Nations AIDS agency, commemorated the day by making a speech in Francistown. He applauded President Mogae's efforts to fight AIDS in his country, not only by developing one of the world's most advanced AIDS treatment plans, but also by speaking out about the disease to his own countrymen and to others in hard-hit southern Africa.

Since 1996 the Botswana Center for Human Rights has held an annual human rights film festival in Gaborone. Beginning in 2002 this has taken place in conjunction with the Maitisong Festival. The films featured in 2005 showcased events taking place in contemporary southern Africa, one about the indigenous !Kung of Botswana and another documenting the HIV/AIDS crisis that still plagues southern Africa.

FOOD

BOTSWANA'S SEMI-ARID CLIMATE limits the country's agricultural potential, but certain crops thrive in those conditions. Batswana grow a wide variety of vegetables and cereal grains, particularly sorghum and millet. The meat provided by cattle ranching remains an important food source. Traditional dishes remain popular in the cities and towns as well, with both street vendors and restaurants offering them to consumers.

Although Botswana remains one of Africa's economic and political success stories, poverty and hunger remain a problem. Approximately 23 percent of children under 5 do not have enough to eat to meet their basic nutritional needs. During 2004–05, a drought occurred that further decreased the country's food supply. The government responded by giving government-sponsored meals to school children and providing income support to needy families through a public works program, which would allow them to purchase imported food from local markets.

Above: **A man harvests sorghum. Sorghum is a commonly grown crop in Botswana.**

Opposite: **Fruit sellers display their produce by the side of a road in Gaborone.**

TYPICAL BATSWANA FOOD

Many traditional Batswana still live by eating the meat from the cattle they raise, the vegetables and grains they grow on small farms, and the edible fruits and tubers found in the bush. Subsistence farming remains a way of life for a large minority of Batswana, including the San and the Herero as well as the Tswana.

BITLONG In traditional villages men tend to be the primary hunters and women the main gatherers. However, women may join the men on extended hunting trips, to care for other animals taken on the trip, and to gather fruits and nuts in new areas. In addition, women traditionally prepare *bitlong* with the meat from the kill. *Bitlong* means "stripped buttock" in Tswana and refers to the custom of curing meat in strips, both to preserve it and to make it easier to carry on long trips.

SORGHUM Among the most plentiful crops in Botswana is sorghum. A tropical cereal grass, sorghum is the fifth major cereal crop in the world, after wheat, rice, corn, and barley. It has an extensive root system and a unique ability to stop growing during times of drought, which makes it particularly appropriate to growing in semi-arid lands such as Botswana. Batswana, traditionally, ferment the sorghum. The fermentation involves the use of lactic acid bacteria, similar to those used to make yogurt, which helps to kill dangerous bacteria and to preserve the food. In addition to porridge, Batswana also use sorghum to make wholegrain products such as breads, pancakes, and dumplings.

DITLOO Another local staple is the *ditloo*, or Bambara groundnut. Similar to the common peanut, the *ditloo* is a legume with very high nutritional components. It contains about 15 to 25 percent protein, 4.5 to 7.4 percent fat, and about 50 percent carbohydrates. Batswana eat them fresh or grill them over a hot fire. Mature *ditloo* become very hard and require boiling in water to soften them. Some Batswana crush the nuts into a paste and then, after adding water, turn it into a porridge.

Strips of *bitlong* are cut into bits to be packaged for sale.

MONGONGO In the Kalahari desert, the !Kung favor another type of legume, the *mongongo*, which makes up about one-third of the total calories consumed by the !Kung. It has a skin covering an edible fruit that has a dry, spongy texture. The taste of the fruit is similar to that of a date, although not as sweet. In the past, the !Kung ate the flesh raw and whole, but now tend to cook it in an iron pot for about 20 minutes.

Below the fruit is the shell of the nut, which is quite hard and difficult to crack. Inside the shell is the nut, which looks like a small hazelnut and tastes like a cashew or almond. If roasted, the nut develops a flavor similar to an aged cheese. The !Kung roast the nut over coals until the shell softens. They eat the nuts whole, sometimes mixed with vegetables, or they grind the nuts into a paste by crushing them with a mortar.

A *tsama* melon growing ripe on the vine.

TSAMA MELON Another common food in the Kalahari is the *tsama* melon. The melon is a major source of both food and water. Round and pale green or yellow in color, the melons are easy to find and collect. Batswana eat the melons seeds after roasting them. The flesh of the fruit is white in color, hard, and tends to be fairly bitter, though sweeter in the center. A related melon found in the Kalahari is the bitter melon, which is always cooked to improve its taste.

MOPANI WORM For hundreds of years, the *mopani* worm has formed a staple in the diets of southern Africans, including Batswana, the !Kung, and the Herero in Botswana. Named after the Mopane tree upon which

they feed, the worms are actually the caterpillars of the emperor moth. The prime *mopani* season is from November to January. Traditionally, women and children are responsible for harvesting the worms by plucking them from the lower branches of the trees. Once harvested, the worms are cooked, either by simmering them with water and vegetables or fried. Many Batswana also enjoy the worms dried, and eat them as snacks like potato chips. *Mopani* worms are very nutritious, containing high levels of protein, calcium, and iron.

FRUITS AND VEGETABLES About 20 percent of Botswana's vegetables—primarily corn, spinach, onions, tomatoes, and cabbage—are grown in the country for local consumption and the rest are imported from other countries, particularly South Africa. Fruits include oranges, peaches, mangoes, and bananas. Some vegetables grow in the wild on a seasonal basis, including the leaves of bean plants that many Batswana eat after drying.

COOKING THE BOTSWANA WAY

Seswaa, also known as *chotlho*, is a very popular traditional meat dish served at most special occasions. Traditionally, men cook *seswaa* using a three-legged iron pot and simmer the meat until soft in salted water. Another popular dish is *serobe*, which consists of the intestines and organs of goat, sheep, or cow that are cooked until soft. Chicken is also a popular food. Tswana families often serve chicken to guests in order to show special hospitality. Except for an occasional sprinkle of chili pepper, the chicken is cooked with only salt and water. Cooking the chicken over open fire in a three-legged cast iron pot gives it the best taste.

A main staple of the Batswana diet is *bogobe*, a porridge made with sorghum, corn, or millet. Because it is inexpensive and nutritious, many traditional families depend on *bogobe* to survive. Batswana make *bogobe* by putting the grain into boiling water, stirring it into a soft paste, and then cooking it slowly. Another way of making *bogobe* is to add sour milk. The Kalanga make a fermented porridge dish, called *tophi*, to which they add melon. *Ting*, eaten by Batswana on special occasions such as weddings and holidays, is a sweet version of the dish made with fermented milk and sugar.

Bread flour is not part of the basic Batswana diet, but Botswana has imported it for years and several bread recipes have become part of the national food. The most common are made with dough (a mixture of water and flour) and cooked with oil. Batswana used dough to make dumplings (called *matemekwane*), flat cakes (*diphaphatha*), and fat cakes (*magwinya*). These are served with spiced meat and vegetables.

DRINKS

Many soft drinks are made in factories in Botswana, including Coca-Cola and Fanta. A favorite non-alcoholic homemade drink is ginger beer, which Batswana enjoy at large ceremonies such as weddings and funerals. The main ingredients of ginger beer are ground ginger, tartaric acid, cream of tartar, and sugar. Usually the drink is flavored with pineapple, raisins, or fresh oranges.

Botswana also offers several types of traditionally-produced alcoholic beverages. *Bojalwa ja Setswana*, the beer of the Tswana, is brewed from fermented sorghum seeds. Other groups, such as the Kalanga, use millet instead of sorghum to make beer. *Chibuku* is a commercially-produced and packaged beer made from either corn or sorghum. *Chibuku* is also brewed in other neighboring countries, including Malawi, South Africa, Zambia, and Zimbabwe. *Khadi*, which is brewed from various ingredients including wild berries, is another widely consumed alcoholic beverage.

A man kneads bread dough, which is mostly used for making fried breads, dumplings, and flat cakes.

NUTRITION AND AIDS

Proper nutrition is an essential component of treatment for HIV/AIDS infections. Studies cited in a special report by the South Africa Institute of National Affairs reveal how essential a proper diet is to someone suffering from the virus. A study published in the July 2005 issue of the *New England Journal of Medicine*, for instance, found that death rates among HIV-positive patients who received a daily multivitamin tablet containing vitamins B, C and E were significantly lower than those who did not.

Unfortunately, eating enough of the right kinds of food is difficult for many poor Batswana. "The problem with the whole nutritional argument is that everyone talks about how everyone must have a well-balanced diet," said Basil Kransdorff, founder of Econocom Foods, which produces a nutrient-heavy food supplement used by many HIV-positive people in Botswana and across the continent. "If you're sitting in a squatter camp and are poor, it's like telling them to fly."

The Botswana government operates Africa's most advanced prevention and treatment plan, but experts agree that in order to fully address the needs of HIV and AIDS patients, more attention needs to be paid to making sure that all Batswana have adequate access to food and supplements.

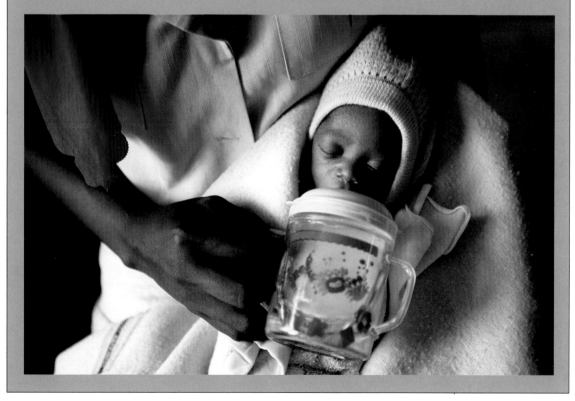

SESWAA (POUNDED MEAT)

This dish is made by cooking meat in a three-legged cast iron pot using only salt and water; adding other spices is taboo. Once the meat is tender and soft, the cook uses wooden spoons to chop it up into bite-sized pieces.

2 pounds (1 kg) beef or other meat (preferably the tender breast meat or brisket)
water
1 large onion, chopped
salt to taste
pepper to taste

Place the meat, onion, and spices in a saucepan. Cover with water and cook about two hours until soft. Drain liquid and pound the meat until flaky. Remove the bones. Serve with *bogobe* (porridge), *morogo*, which are green leafy vegetables cooked with spices, and gravy.

BOGOBE (PORRIDGE)

Bogobe is a simple porridge made with sorghum, or corn flour and water that is one of the staples of the Batswana diet. Many Batswana choose to ferment the porridge by first soaking the grain in water or sour milk. Almost anything can be added to *bogobe*, including vegetables, sugar, and spices. Here is the basic recipe:

2 tablespoons (30g) corn flour (usually sold as *masa harina*)
1 cup buttermilk
6 cups (1.5 liters) of water

Mix two tablespoons of corn flour with sour milk in a pot. Cover the pot and leave the mixture to ferment for 24 hours. Add the fermented meal to six cups of boiling water and cook for 15 minutes.

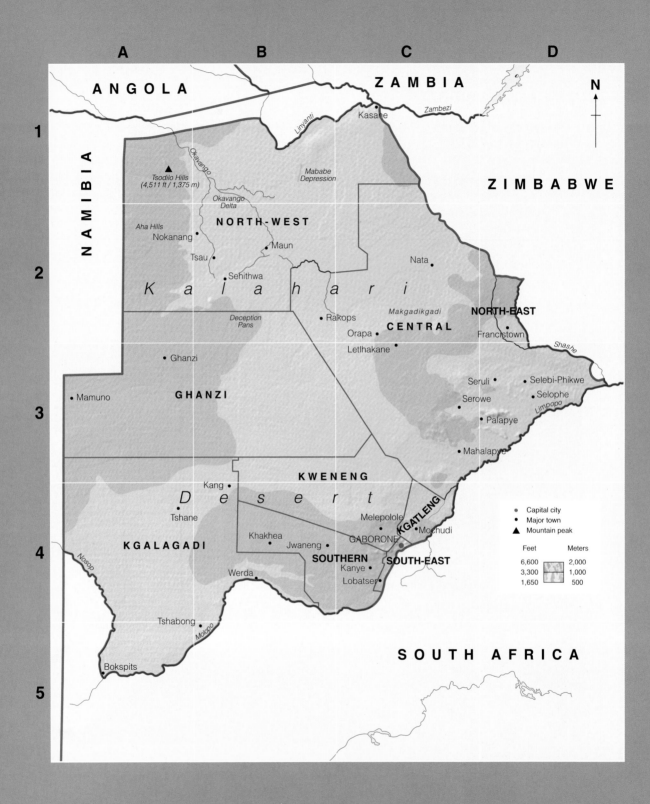

MAP OF BOTSWANA

ECONOMIC BOTSWANA

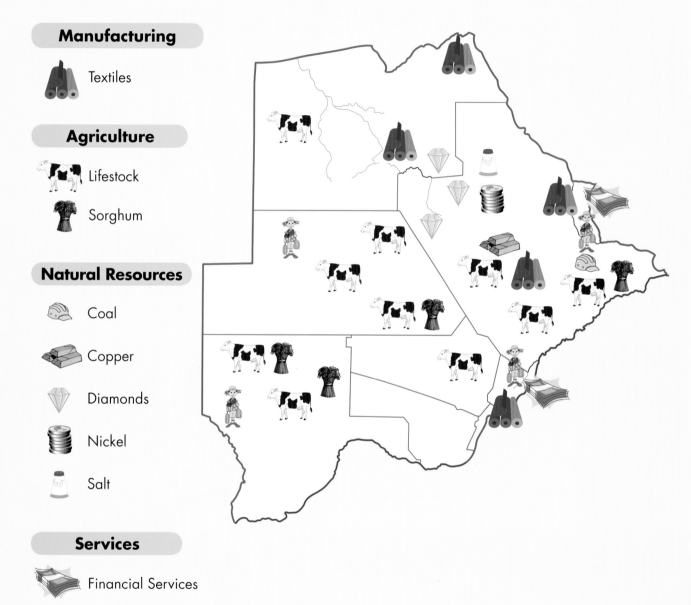

Manufacturing

Textiles

Agriculture

Lifestock

Sorghum

Natural Resources

Coal

Copper

Diamonds

Nickel

Salt

Services

Financial Services

Tourism

ABOUT THE ECONOMY

OVERVIEW
Since 1966, when it attained its independence from Great Britain, Botswana has continued to foster one of the world's most dynamic and successful economies. Based largely on diamond mining, the Botswana economy also depends on tourism, which flourishes in large part because of the country's remarkable variety of wildlife. However, poverty and unemployment continue to plague the population; it is believed that more than 40 percent of Batswana are unemployed. Although the government continues to work to diversify the economy and increase job growth, it faces an overwhelming challenge in meeting the crisis—to the economy and to the lives of all Batswana—posed by the AIDS crisis.

GROSS DOMESTIC PRODUCT (GDP)
$16.64 billion (2005 estimate)

GDP SECTORS
Diamond mining, tourism, financial services

ECONOMIC GROWTH RATE
4.5 percent (2005 estimate)

CURRENCY
1 pula = 100 thebes
USD 1 = 4.56 pula (February 2006)
Notes: 10, 20, 50, 100 pula
Coins: 1, 2, 5 pula and 5, 10, 25, 50 thebe

POPULATION BELOW POVERTY LINE
47 percent (2002)

LAND AREA
231,743 square miles (600,370 square km)

AGRICULTURAL PRODUCTS
Livestock, sorghum, maize, millet, beans, sunflowers, groundnuts

NATURAL RESOURCES
Diamonds, copper, nickel, soda ash, meat, textiles

MAIN IMPORTS
Foodstuffs, machinery, electrical goods, transport equipment, textiles, fuel, wood and paper products, metal and metal products

MAJOR TRADE PARTNERS
European Free Trade Association (EFTA), South African Customs Union (Lesotho, Namibia, South Africa, Swaziland), Zimbabwe, United States

INTERNATIONAL AIRPORTS
Sir Seretse Khama Internatonal Airport, Gaborone

CULTURAL BOTSWANA

Tsodilo Hills
Located in the western Kalahari, near the border of Namibia, the Tsodilo Hills offer clear evidence that Botswana was inhabited as long ago as 17,000 B.C. A cluster of five hills, the Tsodilo Hills preserves a chronological account of human activities and environmental changes over at least 100,000 years. It is of particular significance to the !Kung, who consider the Tsodilo Hills to be sacred ground.

Nhabe Museum
The only museum located in Botswana's northwest, about two hours away from the Moremi Game reserves, it presents the natural history and culture of the Okavango region with wildlife exhibits and cultural artifacts.

Lesoma Memorial Monument
In 1978 the bitter fight for freedom for blacks living in Rhodesia (Zimbabwe) spilled over Botswana's borders in the Chobe District. Fifteen Batswana soldiers were killed. A monument stands in memory of those soldiers.

Kuru Museum and Cultural Center
Located in the village of D'Kar in the Ghanzi division of Botswana, this center features arts and crafts presented by the local !Kung. Nearly every year, the cultural center hosts a traditional dance festival for youth and adults alike.

Maun Educational Center
Located on the eastern bank of the Thamalakane River near the border of Namibia, this reserve, full of wildlife, including impalas, zebras, wildebeests, and giraffes, offers visitors four different walking trails.

Kgosi Khama III Memorial Museum
Located in Serowe, a village between Gaborone and Francistown, this museum opened in 1985. Its focus is the cultural history of the local !Kung and Bangwato groups. In addition to featuring a gallery, which often features exhibits borrowed from other institutions, the museum provides a permanent display of the three types of Bangwato settlements: the home, the lands, and the cattle post.

Livingstone Memorial
David Livingstone, one of Botswana's first Christian missionaries from Great Britain, and one of history's most remarkable explorers, began to work with Motswana in 1848 when he moved to Kolobeng, just 19 miles (30 km) north of Gaborone. His home, as well as the church he built, are monuments to his work that are open to the public.

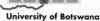

University of Botswana
Founded in 1982, the University of Botswana is the center of higher education in Botswana. It offers faculties in six disciplines, educates about 3,000 students every year, and welcomes Batswana of all ages to many lectures and programs that are open to the public.

National Museum & Art Gallery
When it comes to modern art, the National Museum & Art Gallery in Gaborone is the centerpiece for Botswana. Opened in 1968, it now holds regular exhibitions of local artists. Every April it hosts the annual "Artists in Botswana," which draws hundreds of visitors.

Matsieng Footprints
Located a few miles northeast of Gaborone, the Matsieng Footprints are rock outlines of what the Tswana people believe are the footprints of their ancestor Matsieng. The archaeological site was declared a national monument in 1971.

ABOUT THE CULTURE

COUNTRY NAME
Republic of Botswana (formerly Bechuanaland)

CAPITAL
Gaborone

OTHER MAJOR CITIES
Francistown, Selebi-Phikwe, Mahalapye, Serowe, Molepolole

POPULATION
1,640,115 (2005 estimate)

POPULATION GROWTH RATE
0 percent (2005 estimate)

ADMINISTRATIVE DIVISIONS
Central, Ghanzi, Kgalagadi, Kgatleng, Kweneng, North East, North West, South East, Southern

LIFE EXPECTANCY
33.87 years (2005 estimate)

PEOPLE WITH HIV/AIDS
350,000 (2003 estimate)

LITERACY RATE
79.8 percent (2003 estimate)

ETHNIC GROUPS
Tswana 79 percent; Kalanga 11 percent; Basarwa 3 percent; Other, including Kgalagadi and whites 7 percent

MAJOR RELIGIONS
Christian 79 percent, Badimo 6 percent, Other 1.4 percent, Unspecified 0.4 percent, None 20.6 percent

OFFICIAL LANGUAGES
Setswana 78.2 percent, Kalanga 7.9 percent, Sekgalagadi 2.8 percent, English 2.1 percent (official), others 8.6 percent, unspecified 0.4 percent

MAJOR HOLIDAYS
New Year's Day (January 1), Good Friday (Friday before Easter), Easter (variable), Ascension Day (forty days after Easter), Sir Seretse Khama Day (July 1), President's Day (July 15–16), Botswana Day (September 30–October 1), Christmas (December 25), Boxing Day (December 26)

LEADERS IN POLITICS
Sir Seretse Khama, first president (1966–1980); President Ketumile Masire, first vice president, then president (1984–1998); President Festus Mogae, current president since 1998; Ian Khama, current vice president

TIME LINE

IN BOTSWANA	IN THE WORLD

17,000 B.C.
First known human settlements

753 B.C.
Rome is founded.

116–17 B.C.
The Roman Empire reaches its greatest extent, under Emperor Trajan (98–17).

A.D. 01–1000
Bushmen retreat into the Kalahari desert as the Tswana begin populating Botswana.

A.D. 600
Height of Mayan civilization

1200s
Bantu speakers, including Tswana, move south, settling near Limpopo River.

1530
Beginning of trans-Atlantic slave trade organized by the Portuguese in Africa.

1776
U.S. Declaration of Independence

1789–99
The French Revolution

1867
European gold prospectors arrive.

1861
The U.S. Civil War begins.

1869
The Suez Canal is opened.

1885
British proclaim a protectorate called Bechuanaland.

1914
World War I begins.

1939
World War II begins.

1949
The North Atlantic Treaty Organization (NATO) is formed.

1950
Chief of the Ngwato, Seretse Khama, is deposed and exiled by the British.

1952
Batswana rioters protest Khama's exile.

1957
The Russians launch Sputnik.

1960
Bechuanaland People's Party (BPP) is established; Britain approves new constitution. Executive Council, Legislative Council, and African Council are established.

1965
Seretse Khama becomes prime minister.

IN BOTSWANA	IN THE WORLD
1966 Bechuanaland is granted independence and becomes Republic of Botswana with Seretse Khama as president.	**1966–69** The Chinese Cultural Revolution
1967 Diamonds discovered at Orapa	
1980 Botswana is founding member of Southern African Development Coordination Conference (SADCC). President Seretse Khama dies. Quett Masire is made president.	**1986** Nuclear power disaster at Chernobyl in Ukraine **1991** Break-up of the Soviet Union
1995 Government relocates thousands of Bushmen to settlements outside Central Kalahari Game Reserve.	**1997** Hong Kong is returned to China.
1998 Masire resigns as president and retires. Festus Mogae, former vice president, becomes president under new rules of constitution.	
2000 Devastating floods destroy the homes of more than 20,000 Batswana. President Mogae announces that AIDS drugs will be made available free of charge.	**2001** Terrorists crash planes in New York, Washington, D.C., and Pennsylvania.
2002 Kalahari Bushmen take the government to court to challenge the forced eviction from their land; the case is dismissed on a technicality.	
2003 Botswana erects a fence along its border with Zimbabwe to keep out illegal immigrants.	**2003** War in Iraq
2004 HIV infection rate falls to 37.96 percent; Botswana no longer has the world's highest infection rate. Workers at largest diamond-mining company strike over wages. President Mogae wins a second term in elections.	

GLOSSARY

AIDS
Acquired Immunodeficiency Syndrome, an incurable disease of the immune system caused by an infection with a virus. Botswana has among the highest rates of AIDS in the world.

apartheid
System of government that separates people on the basis of race and deprives one or more groups of important civil rights.

badimo (bah-DI-mo)
Ancestral spirits in the Tswana religion.

Batswana (singular, Motsana)
Name for all people who live in Botswana.

indigenous
Something that occurs naturally in a particular region or area, including people, animals, and plants.

Kgalagadi (gall-ah-GADEE)
In Setswana, the Kalahari desert.

kgosi (GO-si)
A Tswana chief.

!Kung (KOON)
The name of the Botswana's earliest settlers who have lived on the Kalahari desert for centuries. Also called the San or Bushmen.

lekgapho (lek-GAP-ho)
Traditional Tswana murals.

letsema (let-SEE-ma)
Voluntary work performed by members of a group on behalf of a family.

mafisa (ma-FEE-sa)
Tswana system of sharing cattle with needy villagers.

mephato (mef-FAT-oh)
In traditional Tswana culture, a regiment of young men who could be called upon by their villages to perform community activities.

Merafe (morafe, plural; mer-raf-ee)
A Tswana chiefdom.

n!ore
A Bushmen hunting and gathering territory.

ngaka (na-GAH-kah)
A traditional healer.

patlo
A marriage agreement.

salt pan
Expanses of ground in the desert covered with salt and other minerals.

savanna
A treeless plain.

sebaga (se-BAY-ga)
Traditional Tswana one-stringed instrument.

FURTHER INFORMATION

BOOKS

Aiken, Bruce. *The Lions and Elephants of the Chobe: Botswana's Untamed Wilderness.* New York: Book Sales, 1987.

Bailey, Adrian and Robyn Keene Young. *Wild Botswana.* Cape Town: Sunbird, 2000.

Leith, J. Clarke. *Why Botswana Prospered.* Montreal: McGill-Queen's University Press, 2005.

Owens, Mark and Cordelia Dykes Owens. *Cry of the Kalahari.* New York: Houghton Mifflin, 1992.

Smith, Alexander McCall. *The Girl Who Married a Lion and Other Tales from Africa.* New York: Pantheon, 2004.

Swaney, Deana; Mary Fitzpatrick; Paul Greenway; Andrew Stone; and Justine Vaisutus. *Lonely Planet Southern Africa.* Melbourne: Lonely Planet, 2003.

WEBSITES

Birdlife Botswana. www.birdlifebotswana.org.bw/

Botswana Tourism and General Information. www.botswanatourism.org.uk

Botswana Television. www.btv.gov.bw/

Central Intelligence Agency World Factbook (select Botswana from the country list) www.cia.gov/cia/publications/factbook

Daily News Online. www.gov.bw/cgi-bin/news.cgi

Government of Botswana. www.gov.bw/home.html

HIV and AIDS in Botswana. www.avert.org/aidsbotswana.htm

Mmegi. Botswana's weekly newspaper. www.mmegi.bw

University of Botswana. www.ub.bw/

Wildcam Africa (live pictures from Botswana and other African countries) http://www9.nationalgeographic.com/ngm/wildcamafrica/wildcam.html

VIDEOS

Botswana Safari. Westlake Entertainment, 1998.

The Gods Must be Crazy. Fox Home Entertainment, 1992.

BIBLIOGRAPHY

Biesele, Megan, and Kxo Royal. *San*. New York: The Rosen Group, 1997.

Bolaane, Maitseo and Part T. Mgadla. *Batswana*. New York: The Rosen Group, 1997.

Lauré, Jason. *Botswana*. Chicago: The Children's Press, 1993.

Udechukwu, Ada. *Herero*. New York: The Rosen Group, 1996.

INDEX